Writers of Wales

CW00516985

Editors
MEIC STEPHENS   R. BRINLEY JONES

Kate Holman

BRENDA CHAMBERLAIN

University of Wales Press

Cardiff 1997

I

I had, at about the age of six, decided to be a painter and writer, declared Brenda Chamberlain. Having designed the pattern of her life, she followed it faithfully to the end.

Her childhood was spent in Bangor: on one side the sombre grandeur of the mountains of Snowdonia; on the other the Menai Straits leading out to the Irish Sea. There she grew up with her younger brother Neville, and many years later remembered the adventures that gripped her infant imagination:

> *The tank at the top of the garden . . . was full of scummy, foul-smelling water. This for me was Africa where, I told my brother for impression's sake, I had been born. I lied and lied, about the heat, crocodiles, swamps. Alligators turned in strong, smooth waters. My brother was sick with envy and admiration. The garden was enclosed by a slate fence. I drew on the slates with fragments of stone, which gradually made me aware of texture and colour.*
>
> (ARTISTS IN WALES, Gwasg Gomer, 1971)

Brenda Chamberlain's family had settled in Bangor by the time she was born on 17 March 1912. Her father, an Inspector of Bridges for the London, Midland and Scottish Railway, came from Hill Ridware, near Lichfield in England, and was distantly related to the former Prime Minister Neville Chamberlain. Her mother's parents were of Manx and Irish origin, and their family name Cooil was distinctively Manx.

Her mother Elsie Chamberlain was an exceptionally strong-willed and capable woman, ready to fight for her socialist ideals and fierce belief in equal rights for women. She became the town's first woman mayor. Mrs Chamberlain had high aspirations for her gifted daughter, and found great satisfaction in her successes. Her father Francis Thomas Chamberlain, by contrast, was a quiet, retiring man; a bee-keeper and former church sidesman. He could adopt a cynical manner which sometimes made Brenda unhappy.

Her education started at kindergarten and preparatory school *under the mothering arm of Bangor University College*:

From those days, I remember no restraints at all, only encouragement to dress up, dance (it was the time of Rhythmic Movements), paint pictures on a real easel, write essays and poems.

So when she reached Bangor County School for Girls, the constraints of uniform and 'ladylike' behaviour were hard to accept. In Maths she was *unteachable*, but showed such ability in Art that she was sent for special lessons at the Royal Cambrian Academy in Conwy. She wrote poetry, and in her last school year adopted her own timetable of English, Art and Languages.

After leaving school Brenda Chamberlain spent six months in Copenhagen as an au pair. It was her first experience of life in a capital city, and in a foreign country. But the greatest impression of all was made by her first encounter with modern art. She was enthralled by Paul Gauguin's early paintings of Brittany at the Karlsberg Glyptotekh, and this work was to have a lasting influence. In Copenhagen, wandering fearlessly along quaysides and through gardens, she made drawings which helped, on her return, to win her a place at the Royal Academy Schools in London in 1931.

Among Brenda Chamberlain's fellow students in the painting school was a young artist – two years her junior – named John Petts. About half-way through her five-year training they found a studio flat together in Redcliffe Road, South Kensington. He remembered:

She was an original – she had a quality of genius. I had never met anyone like that, and she seemed like a breath of fresh air. She was full of the love of things; always smiling. She was a wraith from the hills.

She seemed to float down the vaulted corridors of the Royal Academy, dressed in a long white overall with a broad collar, like a nun's habit, said John Petts. Her long, angular face was framed by flowing golden hair. And she talked passionately: about people, about art, but most of all about her native mountains of north Wales. In the spring of 1935 they were married in Kensington.

The following year they returned to Wales together, to Brenda Chamberlain's mountains. She found a pair of disused drovers' cottages situated high above the village of Rachub, near Llanllechid in northern Caernarfonshire, set among the dark slate quarries around Bethesda and the towering mountains of Snowdonia. The property cost £68, and they renovated it painstakingly themselves. They called their new home Tŷ'r Mynydd, the Mountain House. Both were fiercely idealistic and determined to earn their living by their art.

Under the influence of D. H. Lawrence, we hated the machine.
We had outlawed ourselves, though we had never heard of 'beat'
or 'off-beat'. We never drank alcohol, and we had never heard of
narcotics. Free love was our creed and password.
(ALUN LEWIS AND THE MAKING OF THE CASEG BROADSHEETS)

Their lifestyle was primitive and rigorous, both physically and morally, for Brenda Chamberlain set ruthlessly high standards for herself and for others. She wrote:

Quite frankly, I loathe contact with most people. I like men and women and children who are vital, standing alone in their own world, and not dependant [sic] on others for their happiness.
(Letter to Alun Lewis, 15 June 1941)

We lived like peasants, we tramped the hills, really elevated and excited, recalled John Petts. *We got to know every inch of Snowdonia.* Brenda Chamberlain was considered eccentric by many in those pre-war days. She dressed in long, loose skirts and big-brimmed hats, and Petts had a long beard. Their animals included a pony named Polly on which she rode down into Bangor to shop, with her husband by her side, earning themselves the nickname 'Mary and Joseph'. They became *obscure rebels, detached from the world* ('How the Caseg Broadsheets began', 1962).

They bought a simple Adana printing machine, and produced hand-coloured greetings cards from their bold woodcuts and engravings. It was dubbed the Caseg Press, after the mare, and the Caseg River which flowed near the cottage. Meanwhile, both strove to articulate their individual artistic visions, and their first joint exhibition was in Bangor in 1937.

4

But as Petts achieved more recognition, the rivalry between them grew.

Brenda Chamberlain started writing journals, which she filled with sketches and notes of her impressions; particularly of the mountains she both loved and feared:

The wind tortures the walls of our cottage and sends the snow in soft rushes like flung sand against the windows. The little panes are nearly all choked white-over now – and we shall not know how high the snow stands in the morning. Terrible flashes of blue lightning play constantly at the windows. In what a fear they put me. It is as if we are wrapped in flickering blue flames here and can never get out of this bewitched cottage.

The coming of war in 1939 brought an end to this life. John Petts became a conscientious objector and started work at Addlestead Farm in Epsom, Surrey. Brenda Chamberlain stayed in Snowdonia, working as a mountain guide for the Red Cross. She looked after John Petts's much younger brother Peter, *a strange child, quiet, unnaturally thin, intensely imaginative, and with beautiful eyes.* He was the first of a series of children she became strongly attached to, and throughout her life she often seemed happiest in the company of young people.

At the beginning of the war an unexpected letter arrived at Tŷ'r Mynydd from the young soldier poet Alun Lewis. On 14 April 1941 he wrote proposing they should work together on a series of inexpensive broadsheets, comprising poems and engravings. John Petts and Brenda Chamberlain were caught up by his enthusiasm. Between November 1941 and June 1942, six Caseg Broadsheets were printed (although the Caseg Press itself was too primitive for the job) in editions of 500. Brenda Chamberlain met Alun Lewis only once, in October 1941, when he stopped in Llanllechid on his way from training camp in Morecambe to visit his wife Gweno's family in Aberystwyth.

In 1943, John Petts and Brenda Chamberlain separated. A significant element in the rift was her ruthless determination to achieve recognition as an artist in her own right. *I realise that any kind of success complicates a relationship*, said John Petts. *She was a great egotist. Brenda had her own straight line, imaginative and romantic.* The break, together with Alun Lewis's departure for India in 1942, and death in March 1944, meant the end of the broadsheets.

Brenda Chamberlain spent some time with her friend Esme Firbank on her sheep farm Dyffryn Mymbyr on the slopes of the Glyders.[1] And she visited friends in Scotland. She had not painted since the outbreak of the war and was working instead on poetry, which began to achieve success. Her first published poem was 'The Harvesters' in THE WELSH REVIEW (October 1939). During the 1940s, her articles and poems appeared regularly in periodicals in Wales, England, Ireland, America and Italy.

As a girl of twenty, Brenda Chamberlain had met a young German who was visiting Bangor, Karl von Laer. They exchanged letters after he returned to his law studies in Königsberg, although contact was lost

[1] The story of Dyffryn Mymbyr is told by Thomas Firbank in I BOUGHT A MOUNTAIN (George Harrap, 1940). Esme, later Mrs Kirby, took over the farm from her husband.

6

during the war when he fought on the Russian Front. As the years passed this relationship became more and more significant to her, personally and artistically. They renewed their correspondence after the war. Von Laer had abandoned his family estate in the eastern zone and was a refugee in the Westphalian 'water castle' (moated farmhouse) of his cousins.

Another crucial event occurred in 1946. During the war Brenda Chamberlain had met a young German, Henry Michalski, who came to England in the 1930s as an exile from Hitler's persecution, and adopted the name Mitchell. He took her on a two-day visit to Ynys Enlli, the island of Bardsey, in the Irish Sea six miles off the Llŷn Peninsula. She fell in love with it instantly:

Listen: I have found the home of my heart. I could not eat: I could not think straight any more; so I came to this solitary place and lay in the sun.

(TIDE-RACE)

A year later she settled there with a Frenchman, Jean van der Bijl, some nine years younger than her. They lived in the large, two-storey, eaveless farmhouse, Carreg, built in the nineteenth century from the stones of the old abbey. The tiny, isolated community consisted of only about a dozen people. The life was hard: fishing, hunting rabbits and farming the few fertile acres between the mountain, with its bleak wall of rock turned against the mainland, and scrubland at the island's southern tip. There were no roads and there was no electricity. Essentials such as flour and paraffin had to be ferried across the treacherous Sound, and boats dragged laboriously from the sea in all weathers.

7

But on Ynys Enlli Brenda Chamberlain's work as an artist and writer flourished. In the large sunlit rooms she decorated the walls with her own murals. She developed a distinctive new style of painting: bold figures in oil, absorbing influences of Gauguin, Picasso and Matisse, which won her Gold Medals at the National Eisteddfod in 1951 and 1953. Exhibitions in London and around the country were praised by critics. Her collection of poems, THE GREEN HEART, won an award from the Welsh Committee of the Arts Council of Great Britain in 1956 and was published by Oxford University Press in 1958.

In the summer, Carreg was filled with visitors, including artists and writers such as Stephen Spender, who brought his children with him. Brenda Chamberlain made frequent trips to London, visited Karl von Laer in Germany, and her art dealer Charles Gimpel's family in Menerbes in the south of France. In 1971 she wrote of Bardsey: *The fifteen years spent there were the most splendid (so far) of my life.*

But by the late 1950s she began to tire of the storms and solitude. Jean had begun teaching French on the mainland, where he settled in 1958. After this, she spent only the summers at Carreg. She searched for a new direction in life. In 1962 TIDE-RACE was published to a chorus of literary acclaim. It was a vivid, haunting account of life on Ynys Enlli. But some of the islanders were deeply offended by her portrayal of them. When she finally gave up Carreg in 1964 it was at the request of the owner, Lord Newborough.

Even before her farewell to Bardsey, Brenda Chamberlain had begun to lay the foundations for the next phase of her life. In August 1962 she accepted a lift to Athens with a male friend. Already her poems reflected a growing fascination with the Mediterranean, the *fountain head* of her own Welsh sea. *The Mediterranean washed my dreams.*

The following year she returned to the island of Ydra, to stay in a house borrowed from a friend, in a Greek peasant village under the mountains at the head of the Kala Pigadhia, the 'good wells'. Henry Mitchell also had a house on the island. It was to be her home, on and off, for the next five years. In 1964 her only 'novel', THE WATER-CASTLE, was published, but was less successful than TIDE-RACE.

In Greece she met a dancer named Robertus Saragas and started to work with him. They wrote 'collaborative poems' like 'Stars shine in the field' and 'Let the wind blow'. He set choreography to her verse, and she made drawings of his movements. *The first tentative drawings were naturalistic . . . then they became stylised . . . I began to feel that these signs were moving.* The outcome was a Dance Recital performed at the Lamda Theatre in London in November 1964, combining poetry by Brenda Chamberlain and Michael Senior, read by Dorothy Tutin, the dancing of Robertus Saragas and Nahami Abbell, music by Debussy and Bach and Judaic folksongs.

Brenda Chamberlain undertook a similar experiment with a composer, Halim El-Dabh. She 'drew' his music 'Theodora in Byzantium' 'automatically', without watching her hand at work. She felt it stemmed from a kind of *psychic experience; a direct inspiration from him to me.* Such possibilities of extra-sensory communication appealed to her throughout her life. Her account of life on Ydra, A ROPE OF VINES, appeared in 1965 subtitled 'Journal from a Greek Island'.

Brenda Chamberlain spent the early part of 1967 in Bangor where her mother – now in her eighties – was transferred to a home for elderly people. She returned to Greece, but her life there was never the same. Within a week, the Greek Colonels carried out their brutal *coup d'état.*

After months of despair and artistic sterility, Brenda Chamberlain wrote a play, THE PROTAGONISTS, *at white-heat in three weeks.* Provoked by a visit to the island of Leros with its political detention centre, it was written *for Greece.* Two copies were sent home via Cyprus, and with a third hidden in a shoulder-bag she left Greece for good in November 1967, *as a voluntary exile.*

THE PROTAGONISTS was performed the following October by the Welsh Drama Studio in the Pritchard Jones Hall of the University College, Bangor. But a bid to take the play to Coventry, Cambridge or London failed through lack of funds. Plans for a London art exhibition also fell through.

Such disappointments took their toll on Brenda Chamberlain. She was now fifty-six – back in Bangor where she had started. She found it hard to work, being without the inspiration and excitement of new experiences, and money grew short. She was no longer surrounded by friends – and dreaded loneliness. She worked laboriously on a new play or film script entitled 'A One-legged Man takes a Walk', and tried to sell some of her *precious* German notebooks to the Welsh Arts Council, but angrily rejected what she considered to be a paltry offer.

Under these pressures, in 1969, Brenda Chamberlain had a nervous breakdown, and spent a short time in hospital. For a while, after this, things got better. POEMS WITH DRAWINGS (1969) and ALUN LEWIS AND THE MAKING OF THE CASEG BROADSHEETS (1970) were published by the Enitharmon Press, and a touring exhibition held. She was gratified by invitations to take part in the Welsh Arts Council's 'Dial-a-poem' and 'Writers in Schools' projects. She struggled with yet another play, 'The Monument', based on the life of the Greek composer Mikis Theodorakis. And at Christmas 1970 she made her last visit to the von Laers, without enthusiasm. Here too perhaps, she was being forced to accept cold reality, instead of the romance she had treasured for so long.

During moods of artistic frustration and great depression she was encouraged by friends to draw anything that came into her head. She executed a series of fragile, psychologically telling sketches of a young woman; bound, or weighted, or rooted to the ground. These were exhibited at the University of Wales centre at Gregynog during May 1971. In June she recorded 'Why did you ring me?' for 'Dial-a-poem':

> Out there, how does it feel?
> are there bars in front of your face? . . .
>
> If I could comfort you, then
> I would offer comfort
> but times are harder now
> than they were in my youth . . .

The bars of her own prison were closing in, and things were indeed harder.

On 11 July 1971 Brenda Chamberlain died, after taking eighteen sleeping tablets. Three days earlier she had arrived at the door of her neighbour Ann Cooke and announced: *I have done a very foolish thing. This is a 'cri de cœur'*. She was rushed to the Caernarfon and Anglesey Hospital, but never regained consciousness. Accidental death was the inquest verdict.

All who knew Brenda Chamberlain describe her as fundamentally 'different', vital and original. She was exceptionally gifted, and dedicated to her art.

Her tiny, boyish frame (under five feet tall) was unexpectedly tough and strong. She was ready to throw herself into anything, although opinions vary widely about her practical skills. To some people she appeared distinctly feminine: even when she dressed in slacks and boots, for example, her hands were 'always immaculate'. Others found her lacking in any sexuality, like a child.

Her face was 'Gothic', with a long bony jaw, heavy forehead and aquiline nose. Friends describe her as kind, loving and extremely loyal. Her conversation was brilliant, vivid and absorbing. She combined maturity, self-possession – even sophistication – with an untarnished innocence. Deeply sensitive and idealistic, she never learnt to *cope easily with a rough world*, says Jonah Jones. Her nature was fervent, self-consciously superstitious, and profoundly fatalistic. She wrote in ARTISTS IN WALES: *There is a pattern in life, strong links we form are never really broken;* and in her writing she wove that pattern according to her own unique design.

II

Your Green Heart reads extremely well, Brenda. You've made a big mark with that, I feel, wrote Alun Lewis in 1942. Her early poetry showed a *simplicity* that was *cool and soothing, . . . a kind of innocence . . . something which the accomplished artist almost invariably loses* (letter of 2 June 1941). Brenda Chamberlain was young, uncompromising and full of vigour.

Although THE GREEN HEART was published in London and New York in 1958, she had started writing some of the fifty-two poems at least seventeen years earlier. Their first formulations are found in her early notebooks in the National Library of Wales. Many had already appeared in periodicals, and undergone further refinement through the amendment of words or phrases. She described in TIDE-RACE how she wrote poetry:

I would work at the words, always cutting away; trying to make little express much; condensing, clarifying, and finally forging. Page after page of the notebook would become covered with countless variations of the one poem that might be taken up and laid aside over a period of weeks or months or even years.

The poems fall into two parts. The first twenty-two are individual works, all with a setting either of mountains or sea. The second, more difficult section is 'The Green Heart' cycle itself. It would be convenient for the critic if the rural poems had been written during the war years in Snowdonia, and those of the sea on Bardsey; but this was not the case. Many of the best sea poems, such as 'Lament' and 'Women on the Strand', were composed between 1941 and 1945, before Brenda Chamberlain ever visited the island. For the sea-washed surroundings were already so vividly evoked by her imagination that she 'recognized' Enlli, as soon as she saw it, as her home.

Throughout her life, the sea fascinated and even obsessed her. One image in particular seized her imagination: that of sea-washed bones. It was not new to literature, for instance in Canto IV of 'The Waste Land' by T. S. Eliot, 'Death by Water':

> Phlebas the Phoenician, a fortnight dead,
> Forgot the cry of gulls, and the deep sea swell
> And the profit and loss.
>   A current under sea
> Picked his bones in whispers. As he rose and fell
> He passed the stages of his age and youth
> Entering the whirlpool.
>   Gentile or Jew
> O you who turn the wheel and look to windward,
> Consider Phlebas, who was once handsome and tall as you.

The theme is echoed in Chamberlain's 'Young Fisher Brought to Land':

> When he was cast up
> From the night-fishers' net
> By the Islands of the Dead
> He had long been forgetful
> Of skulls and ships' candles
> Rolling in the sea-way,
> But we who found him, remembered.

She herself drew attention to the influence of Ariel's song in Shakespeare's TEMPEST, which describes metamorphosis by the waves:

> Full fathom five thy father lies;
> Of his bones are coral made;
> Those are pearls that were his eyes:
> Nothing of him that doth fade,
> But doth suffer a sea-change
> Into something rich and strange.

In 'Islandman', Brenda Chamberlain's drowned sailors wear *ropes of pearl round green throats*; and the image of the drowned, transformed into part of the underwater world, appears again and again in these poems:

> The wave tore his bright flesh in her greed:
> My man is a bone ringed with weed.
>
> ('Lament')

Twenty years later, in the 1960s, she began to develop this theme in a series of paintings.

I have lived for years in a world of salt caves, of clean-picked bones and smooth pebbles. I began to paint salt-water drowned man, never completely lost to view . . . In particular there is the breast of the drowned, the man in rock, or the rock-man.

(Catalogue for 'Welsh Drawings', Welsh Committee of the Arts Council of Great Britain exhibition, 1963)

She articulates this haunting death-by-drowning theme through the feelings of those who live close to the sea and draw their livelihood from it; people like the vividly portrayed 'Islandman' himself:

Full of years and seasoned like a salt timber
The island fisherman has come to terms with death.
His crabbed fingers are coldly afire with phosphorus
From the night-sea he fishes for bright-armoured herring;

and his *black-browed wife* who sits at home. Brenda Chamberlain brings to life, powerfully, the defiant young 'Fisherman Husband', or the embittered 'Women on the Strand', who wait for their menfolk to return, their *eyes surf-dimmed from gazing.*

These are dramatic poems, remarkable for the brilliant pictures they create. Throughout her life, the accuracy of her *painter's eye* was matched by an ability to choose precise words to evoke scenes and atmosphere. Images here are skilfully controlled, like the metaphor of the sea as a jealous woman which runs through 'Women on the Strand' and 'Lament', where instead of 'drowning for joy' in the *salt* of his lover's hair, the bridegroom is lustfully devoured by the sea's salt waves.

A contemporary assessment in the HUDSON REVIEW (Vol. XI.ii) described the poems as *pyrotechnic: solid and sensed and strong.* The critic anticipated the very image that was to haunt her: *These are the Aegean islands and these the archaic fishermen of Homer.* He drew a perceptive parallel:

Her Welsh fishing villages have a Mediterranean quality about them; the Furies, the Sirens, are about to appear. I know of no higher compliment.

That *Mediterranean quality* he defined as *an assault upon resignation: a refusal of acceptance.* The poems have a *heroic quality.*

16

No faith attracted Brenda Chamberlain as much as the ancient Greek doctrine of the Fates, and it is this ethos that pervades the poems. It is expressed in Charles Kingsley's well-known poem 'The Three Fishers': *For men must work and women must weep.* These fisherfolk recognize the destined condition of their lives, but they are not submissive. The fisherman defies death in his skill and knowledge of the sea, at once destroyer and provider of life. Each day he throws *his challenge out in lanes of light.* Yet in the end the *death-encounter* cannot be evaded. If their attitude is one of tragic heroism, it is the tragedy of the Greeks rather than of Shakespeare. They are destroyed by the design of Fate.

Was Brenda Chamberlain too indulgently preoccupied with the 'weeping'? She clearly chose melodrama, sorrow and tragedy as the focus for her writing rather than the more humdrum things of life. Her macabre interest in the drowned might be interpreted as morbid, and several of the mountain poems also take death as their theme. In 'Dead Climber', 'Dead Ponies' and 'To Dafydd Coed mourning his mountain-broken dog', the poet contemplates bodies on the mountain – something she must often have done during those war years, working as a mountain guide searching for lost aircraft.

Death's decay provokes a fierce sense of revulsion: the *bodies stink to heaven.* Yet the poet's response is complex, as in the striking introduction of 'Dead Climber':

> *Sheep and goats are blessed that die there*
> *Above the valley bottom.*
> *So now must he be blessed who lies*
> *Broken upon the scree.*

For the climber had his moment of life lived to the ultimate, whereas those below know only empty monotony:

The people of the plain have become shells emptied of delight.
They are broken on wheels of despair
Turning through the endless night of the valley.

He chanced death through a fuller exploration of life. *The blood in him sang once – he was a proper man.* Death, although viewed with horror and pain by his rescuers, holds no more fear for the man who has consummated his existence, and *cast out desire upon the mountain.*

Gwyn Jones, in a contemporary radio review, discerned an *unadorned confident simplicity* in Brenda Chamberlain's poetry, which he likened to Celtic verse. This is demonstrated in the two 'Songs': 'Talysarn' and 'Heron is harsh'. In A CELTIC MISCELLANY (Penguin, 1971) Kenneth Jackson defined the Celtic epigram as a short poem in which an

idea or image is expressed in carefully picked and completely adequate words, to give the maximum of compression and force.

In 'Talysarn' all the hopefulness of youth and the disillusionment of age are compassed in two spare pictures:

> *Bone-aged is my white horse;*
> *Blunted is the share;*
> *Broken the man who through sad land*
> *Broods on the plough.*
>
> *Bone-bright was my gelding once;*
> *Burnished was the blade;*

Beautiful the youth who in green Spring
Broke earth with song.

The alliteration at the beginning of each line is particularly effective, and calls to mind Anglo-Saxon verse such as BEOWULF, as well as the resonance of sound that has always delighted Welsh poets. The influence of Welsh and Anglo-Welsh poetry can be heard in her work. Her pleasure in the arrangement of sounds, and the strange music of her language rhythms, are reminiscent of Gerard Manley Hopkins, who drew on the sound of the Welsh language. And there are momentary echoes of Dylan Thomas, as in 'Christmas Eve': *I lying in the dark awake.*

In 'To Dafydd Coed mourning his mountain-broken dog', the *shepherd friend* confronts death; his cheerful, trusting nature *baffled by crevice and goat height.* He is urged to turn away from the lifeless body which, like his tears, becomes part of the barren stone landscape. This is one of Brenda Chamberlain's finest poems, bringing into the mind's eye the grey, windswept mountainside with its sheep-cropped turf and slithering scree. A complex technique, with phrases and images condensed and hyphenated, still produces a powerfully direct work. One factor is the appropriateness of the theme, taken from personal experience. The mourning shepherd was Dafydd Owen of Coed Uchaf, whose dog was trapped on a ledge and could not be rescued. His son Charles was living in Llanllechid well after the poet's death.

Her poetry is so *engrossed in country Wales* (THE DUBLIN MAGAZINE, April–June 1958) that Alun Lewis urged her to become *less oppressed by mountains.* Yet although in 'Christmas Eve' and 'Shapely peaks well named' the lyrical Welsh names are recited with relish, Brenda Chamberlain did not set out to promote her native country. She declared in 'How the Caseg Broadsheets began':

John and I felt as Vernon Watkins did ('neither nationalist nor national') but put our faith in the individual.

Strands of more exotic imagery – of Germany, the south of France or Greece – are woven through the earthy Welsh texture of her poetry.

The honesty of feeling which characterizes Brenda Chamberlain's writing is both her strength and her weakness. Her artistic themes – primarily love and death – may be universally relevant, but they are articulated always through her own experience.

Here the most personal part of the book, 'The Green Heart' cycle itself, is the least satisfying. 'The Green Heart' was *produced in communication across 'deep water'* with Karl von Laer, to whom the book is dedicated. It tells a story of consuming love and longing. Brenda Chamberlain's great capacity for loving may have lacked an outlet after her break with John Petts. Her idealized relationship with von Laer became the inspiration for poetry, and prose, in THE WATER-CASTLE.

Some of the verses, especially in Parts II and III, remain *verbal gestures* (Douglas Phillips, WESTERN MAIL), identified perceptively by THE DUBLIN MAGAZINE as a personal relief of tension rather than poetry. They lack a measure of objectivity, the seal of *revision in that kernel of peace to which the writer must sometime have access,* as she put it ('Alun Lewis', THE DUBLIN MAGAZINE, July–September 1944).

In the catalogue of her 1970 Welsh Arts Council exhibition 'Word and Image', Brenda Chamberlain again described how some of her poems were *worked on over a period of years.* She regarded the process as mystical, rather than mechanical:

Poetry is too complex a process for me to pin it down. Its roots are too obscure. It really is a great mystery, involving railway stations, lonely shores, strong attachments to place; but out of time, in any strict sense. None of the poems can be dated, therefore.

This account glosses over the craftsmanship employed by even the most eminent of poets. To give just one example, Wordsworth also revised many of his poems, sometimes extensively, so that their composition spanned a number of years. Brenda Chamberlain was capable of skilfully moulding words to achieve the purest form, as shown by 'To Dafydd Coed', and the evolution of 'Rose of Lima' outlined in TIDE-RACE (pp. 182–3). Yet in 'The Green Heart' her touch is less sure. Images are not developed and, like the stag calling for water (Part II.iii), remain merely enigmatic. Other lines adopt the breathless, exclamatory style found in her later work. The NEW YORK TIMES (22 June 1958) criticized much of her verse as *unconvincing writing around poetic objects,* and Anthony Conran claimed it was *never believable as the real utterance of a real woman, but always the fantastic words begotten of an idealizing dream* (THE ANGLO-WELSH REVIEW, Spring 1972). If her mountains and seascapes are idealized to some extent, parts of 'The Green Heart' seem even more the product of dreams:

At Schlotheim, peacocks roosted in branches
No peacocks sit in the Oberbehme willows

Despairing, I have come
To your ancestral home . . .

A ghost shall haunt your rooms
I am honoured guest tonight.

(Part II.i)

Schlotheim was Karl's home in East Germany, to
which he never returned after the war. Brenda
Chamberlain had not been there.

Yet Gwyn Jones recognized the poems as *unusual and
moving*. For some of them capture a sense of loss, the
anguish of bereavement, with poignant and memor-
able insight.

Her poetry *is* 'romantic'. Kenneth Rexroth wrote in
NEW BRITISH POETS in 1949:

*Brenda Chamberlain is, I feel, one of the very few younger poets
who has been able to recapture and transmit or transmute some
of the technical, syntactical, psychological devices and felicities
of those days* [the Twenties] *into the Romantic idiom. She is
one of the poets in Britain whose work I think may . . . presage
the growth of a new post-romantic style.*

His definition of Modern Romanticism as anarchist,
personalist and pacifist highlights the very principles
Chamberlain adhered to. She was a Romantic too in the
more popular sense of the word in that she was
concerned with the expression of personal emotion. Her
work is truly *characterized . . . by imagination and passion*
(SHORTER OXFORD ENGLISH DICTIONARY). Kyffin Williams
sensed in her the

22

anguish of the Romantic, for Brenda seemed uneasy in the world of reality, so that in her fantasies she cut herself off from our world and with the aid of her vivid imagination created a substitute (MABON, Spring 1972).

Part I of 'The Green Heart' draws on Karl von Laer's pre-war letters.

These were the basis of the poetry. This constant, silent dialogue brought me so close to him that though we were far apart in space and in our ways of living, a similarity of temperament and nervous awareness caused the experience of one to become the property of both.

It is a *recreation of his experience as a youth* living in Germany. The poet sees with his eyes and evokes his feelings. 'They say you are thin and weary' was described by Alun Lewis as a *sweet, refreshing poem . . . achieved with such economy of image and word too.* He chose it for the Caseg Broadsheets with part of 'I took no vows', saying *I've chosen the poems that are perfect you see. Others are richer, but more uneven and incomplete* (Letters of August and November 1941).

Parts II and III were written later, and refer to her post-war visits to Westphalia. Brenda Chamberlain herself drew attention to the continuing influence of von Laer's letters. Many of those post-war letters are in the National Library of Wales, and reveal with startling clarity how great that influence was. The 'title' poem itself, 'The Green Heart' Part II.viii:

> *Let me be your Green Heart*
> *Far from you, this difficult way.*
> *The next war may let us die:*
> *Think of me in your last hour.*

comes almost word for word from a letter of February 1953:

Let me be your green Heart, let me go with you in your poetry, this difficult way . . . Perhaps next war let us dy [sic]: then it is good to remember a good friend in the last moment.

The phrase itself was first coined to describe Karl's homeland, Thuringia, the *green heart* of Germany.

Other poems are equally derivative. The last, Part III.xiv:

> *Always remember:*
> *To be loved, is not to be prisoned.*
> *Love flies, over the mountains and the sea,*
> *To where the sun and the stars move.*
> *It is a bird singing in a wood*
> *Under the south wind of springtime.*
> *It is an angel from the hand of God.*

compares with a letter probably written in March 1953:

Often people think to be loved that is to be a prisoner. That's not true: Love, flying over the hills and over the sea, to the sun and the stars, is like an angel coming from the good Lord, like a bird singing in the trees, like the wind, blowing in springtime.

And the last verse of Part II.iii:

> *It is wonderful to be loved; to know the sun,*
> *The high mountains, the sky and the sea,*
> *The day and the night, through one another.*
> *We come home when we are together.*

comes from the February letter:

It is wonderful to be loved. O we love the sun and the mountains, the sea and the sky, the night and the day . . . we can see the same things and hear and feel the same things and therefore, if we are together we are at home.

In an early typescript of THE WATER-CASTLE Brenda Chamberlain also transcribed pre-war letters from her *German friend*. Although there is no guarantee that they are true to von Laer's text, as she amended even the typescript, they undoubtedly contain the essence of his early letters. They include numerous images from Part I of 'The Green Heart'. His *pilgrimage* to the Baltic shore on 24 December, theme of Part I.v and vi (also entitled 'Christmas Eve by the Baltic' and 'Midnight Mass') is recounted in a letter of 1933.

From Oberbehme (the water castle) he writes on 10 December 1946:

The first frost has built a thin bridge of ice over the water which surrounds our house like a small lake. The wild duck living on this water, and that wake us every morning during the summer and autumn with their cries . . . have flown away to the river.

The same image is found in Part I.vii. The German's first letter, from Leipzig in October 1932, contains a description of the city of Amsterdam which Brenda Chamberlain recorded in her May 1941 notebook, and reworked into Part I.i; picturing the *tall patrician houses hung / Upside down in the muddy water of the canals.*

In a letter date-lined Schlotheim, 1 August 1933, he responds to her *tragic feeling*, urging her: *Look up to your beloved mountains.* The exhortation became Part

I.iii, and was published in POETRY QUARTERLY (1945) as 'Reproof from Schlotheim'.

The sources of a writer's inspiration are varied; and many, including Shakespeare, have worked from existing material of one sort or another. Yet I know of no other poet who has taken personal letters and used them, word for word, in this way. In 1973, after her death, the letters were donated anonymously to the National Library of Wales, and held under seal until 1985, when I was given permission to read them.

Brenda Chamberlain herself made no secret of the bond between letters and poems. And Karl von Laer, on the testimony of the early correspondence, expressed only pleasure at her adoption of his ideas; taking it as evidence of their spiritual affinity. The poems become a natural expression of their close relationship.

The more important question is whether the material forms successful poetry. Karl von Laer's letters are spontaneous, moving, courageous; his use of language lyrical. In Brenda Chamberlain's hands the words become more sentimental and self-consciously 'poetic'. Some of the verses, particularly in Part I, are evocative, some well-crafted; but often the emotions within remain second-hand, degenerating into a cloud of brooding, romantic melancholy which obliterates the vividness she achieves elsewhere.

III

Brenda Chamberlain settled on Ynys Enlli in 1947, eager to start a new life:

Can I dare plunge into the hermit-life, into the fisherman farmer's narrow existence?

I, I, I, ram-horned battering at the holy isle, at the mocking-rock of the seal cave in the east; at the sly bays of the south west; at the Merlin-haunted child-sized fields.

What am I? Whence did I come? Whither shall I go? Among rock-bones in the deeps of the muscular ocean?

Old sea, make our hearts fresh!

TIDE-RACE was published fifteen years later, distilled from her journals.[1] Several passages of prose had already appeared in periodicals. The earliest, 'Mountains of Rock', in THE WELSH REVIEW (1945), was written before Chamberlain visited Bardsey, and described the Glyders. Yet the account of sheep-gathering is lifted straight into the setting of the island, with the amendment merely of a word here and there, such as *mountain rim* to *sea rim*. The image reappeared years later in THE PROTAGONISTS.

This practice of taking an incident out of its time and place, and siting it somewhere quite different, is

---

[1] Six notebooks in the NLW, 1947–62, plus 1941 (referring to Scotland). They also relate the characters to their real counterparts.

common in her writing. For instance, lines recorded in a notebook in the early 1950s were used again in a 1970 'Dial-a-poem', as well as in one of her last, unfinished works, 'A One-legged Man takes a Walk'.

All her work is episodic, rather than following a clear narrative sequence. She wrote about experiences in her life that made a strong impression on her, and exploited them to the full, with little regard for their objective chronology. A passage of prose is updated and fitted into a suitable context, as are the early poems in her final collection, POEMS WITH DRAWINGS.

The tale of the wicked king and the sea-queen is drawn from her earlier children's stories, 'The Magic Comb' and 'The Boy and the Simnel Cake' (MSS in the National Library of Wales) and is reminiscent of familiar folk-myths. Brenda Chamberlain's friend Joan Rees in Bangor has a manuscript account of another episode from TIDE-RACE, entitled 'Eira saves my life on the east side while gathering a stray sheep'. Like her poetry, the book was 'forged' together.

It is said that TIDE-RACE was considered by Faber, and read by T. S. Eliot. It was published by Hodder and Stoughton to coincide with an exhibition of her paintings at the Zwemmer Gallery in London. The book was rapturously received by critics as far afield as South Africa and New Zealand, and serialized in the WESTERN MAIL.

The title refers to the treacherous waters which flow between Bardsey and the mainland, but it also establishes the atmosphere of the book:

*Life on this, as on every small island, is controlled by the moods
of the sea; its tides, its gifts, its deprivations.*

All the events are set in the context of the sea's
dominating power and influence. And Edna O'Brien
was right to remark that Brenda Chamberlain *observes
the sea as closely as one would observe the face of a beloved.*

This encompassing ocean is wild, unpredictable and
destructive; bereaving, and yet paradoxically affording
the means of life. It is the central character in TIDE-RACE,
interacting with all others. The formidable Cadwaladr
is *spawned of the sea: thrown up on a weed-hung wave*; and
Sarah – *her mouth, isn't it always open on a gasp of despair?
It is the sea that does it; being too big.* Its cruelty breeds
harshness and melancholy in the islanders, especially
the women who live harrowing lives:

*I have seen her on other nights when we have been returning
over the sea, the shrouded figure standing motionless in a
corner of the cliff: high on the mountainside over the white, the
wine dark red, the mussel blue ramparts. She is not this or that
familiar woman of the island, but a symbol. Monumental in
patience, the woman watches the Sound . . . She has the face of
one haunted by the imminence of death, predicting that she will
be a corpse within these next three years.*

The island women are the same who gazed
tragically out to sea in THE GREEN HEART. Reviewers
again noted a *Mediterranean colouring* (MANCHESTER
EVENING NEWS, 27 September 1962) in TIDE-RACE,
and the same sense of the omnipotence of the Fates.

Brenda Chamberlain is more intent on creating a
Celtic ambience. The Bardsey community was not
the remnant of an ancient island race – although

29

largely Celtic for all that – as its members had come from the Welsh mainland or further afield. Yet Cecil Price drew a telling comparison with Robin Flower's THE WESTERN ISLAND, Tomas ó Crohan's THE ISLAND-MAN and the work of J. M. Synge.

They describe remarkably similar worlds: particularly Synge's RIDERS TO THE SEA, where Maurya the bereaved mother comes to terms with her son's death with the words: *No man at all can be living for ever, and we must be satisfied.* TIDE-RACE is *drenched in Celtic mysticism* (BELFAST TELEGRAPH, 20 September 1962); and Synge's record of his own stay on THE ARAN ISLANDS describes the same respect for omens and the supernatural. The natural and 'super'-natural elements of life do not have the rigid definition assigned to them by our 'sophisticated' society.

Synge also stresses the *life of torment* of the island women, and the men's dexterity developed through a life of constant danger: just as Cadwaladr chances *green immortality in troughs of the tideway* and is protected only by his inspired cunning.

Brenda Chamberlain's islanders also delight in the narration of vivid and far-fetched tales. They have not abandoned the same simple, harsh way of life:

Other men in western isles must have been crouching as we were crouched, on ledges a few feet above the sea, with lines going down into deep water; weathered men and children, sitting in the shadow of the rocks, baiting hooks for bright-scaled fish.

There is another vital aspect of this elusive Celtic quality. I questioned earlier whether Brenda Chamber-

30

lain's writing might be interpreted as morbid. In TIDE-RACE she returns often to the theme of death, particularly death by drowning. She is surrounded by a *dread sea; tenanted by rotting bones; furnished from wrecked vessels.* The reality of a watery death comes to the writer involuntarily: the ringing of a glass at table – bad luck to sea-men – evokes *the eye of a doomed sailor,* or a drawing of a boy swimming becomes against her will *an unknown man about to drown.* Did John Synge feel a little of the same fascination when he wrote of *this background of empty curaghs, and bodies floating naked with the tide?*

Brenda Chamberlain's preoccupation with death was too complex to be dismissed as morbid or indulgent. In one of her early notebooks she wrote a short critical passage about A. E. Housman including these words:

A. E. Housman had the Celtic vision, his mind was tinged with thoughts of the bone that outlives flesh and soul, holding no cheerful and shallow philosophy to beguile the heart. All things Celtic are anathema to many minds. He did not bow to death – he fought it, knowing who would win.

How perfectly this summarizes the attitude of her stubborn Celtic islanders. Brenda Chamberlain's imagination was gripped by the same dramatic vision, which she regarded as beyond the reach of the intellect alone: *anathema* to those who did not share it. It comprised a deep awareness of the darker side of the human situation, embodied in the spirit of the Celtic keen, the soul-rending, pagan lament for the dead. Synge described it in this way:

This grief of the keen is no personal complaint for the death of one woman over eighty years, but seems to contain the whole passionate rage that lurks somewhere in every native of the island. In this cry of pain the inner consciousness of the people seems to lay itself bare for an instant, and to reveal the mood of beings who feel their isolation in the face of a universe that wars on them with winds and seas. They are usually silent, but in the presence of death all outward show of indifference or patience is forgotten, and they shriek with pitiable despair before the horror of the fate to which they all are doomed.

The sense of the past permeates the island. Brenda Chamberlain feels herself lured on by her *sea-ancestors*, to *sink unknowingly into the moulds of our race*. Her sympathetic awareness of the past adds richness and perspective to the book. Bardsey, the Island of Twenty Thousand Saints, was once a place of pilgrimage which is mentioned in the twelfth-century Book of Llandaf. Here a great congregation of holy men came to die and be buried; and the medieval poet Meilyr elected *To wait resurrection* (PENGUIN BOOK OF WELSH VERSE, edited by Anthony Conran, 1967). Their ghosts inhabit the island. When the fields are ploughed, everywhere the ochre-stained bones are turned up to the air, reminding the islanders of their own mortality.

In TIDE-RACE, legend and myth are woven together just as in the Celtic tales of the Mabinogion, and interspersed with everyday events; so that in the mysterious sea-born atmosphere of mists and darkness and wailing voices of sea-birds, they mingle indistinguishably. She tells of the old king of the island with his tin crown. Jealous of his great-niece's son, he sends the boy away to his sister the sea-queen who bewitches him into a seal. For his cruelty he is driven from the island; and indeed the former 'king' Love Pritchard did leave in his old age (R. M.

32

Lockley, 'The Little Islands round Wales', WALES, December 1958).

The folklore of seafaring communities embodies many tales of the human affinity of seals:

> I am a man upon the land,
> I am a selchie in the sea.
>
> ('The Grey Selchie of Sule Skerry',
> OXFORD BOOK OF BALLADS, 1969)

They are said to be the *people of the sea*, for every creature on land has its counterpart beneath the waves. (See David Thomson, THE PEOPLE OF THE SEA, Barrie and Rockliff, 1965.) On Bardsey the wistful seal cow calls irresistibly:

> . . . *she sent messages of desire, that I should give myself to the sea and plumb the cold stillness of water under the rock. I leaned far over into darkening air; and her mild eyes spoke of human feelings. She took me down to my deepest roots nurtured on legend and fantasy.*

Brenda Chamberlain's superstitious nature attunes to the atmosphere of Ynys Enlli, and she welcomes the *friendly ghosts* whose voices fill the deserted farmhouse, Tŷ Bychan. The sense of the supernatural contributes to a feeling of strangeness about her island. The inhabitants are stubbornly Welsh, yet disconcertingly foreign, cut off from all cultural influences. The children, like Cadwaladr's daughter Siani, are wild and primitive. *She seemed to see the world as an animal does.* Chamberlain never makes clear whether the islanders spoke Welsh: she had little of the language herself although her mother was self-taught.

Twm is compared most closely to the original islanders, who abandoned Enlli in the 1920s when the school was closed. Yet here lies the fundamental difference between TIDE-RACE and THE ARAN ISLANDS, stressed by Conran in THE ANGLO-WELSH REVIEW. Brenda Chamberlain's aim was not to observe and describe the life-style of an old and isolated community, as John Synge did, teaching himself Gaelic for a truer understanding. She scorned national distinctions, and regarded Bardsey rather as a microcosm of universal humanity. *Terror. Violence. Greed* are all present. Her islanders are full of vitality: sometimes unstintingly generous, sometimes cruel, and always pragmatic, like Nans who gives instructions from her death-bed on the sale of her calves.

Starry-eyed newcomers become beaten and dis-illusioned by a life *that would raise sea-monsters of hatred and despair.* Yet the author thrives on it, relishing the drama of family feuds, or a birth in the middle of the Sound, and painting a portrait seen as *larger than life* and coloured with *poetic extravagance* (DAILY TELEGRAPH, 21 September 1962).

Indeed, some of the real islanders were shocked by the book. Jane Roberts and her mother Nellie Evans, who later settled near Aberdaron, identify themselves as the characters Eira and Rhiannon. *She must have been in a black mood when she wrote it,* believed Nellie Evans. *Some people said it was a nasty book, nasty about people,* added Jane Roberts.

The characters are there, and she has made a story around them. There's a grain of truth, but she has mixed them up and exaggerated them.

34

Cadwaladr, for instance, is based on Bardsey's own Twm, the postmaster. Yet the real Wolfgang, named Paněc, did indeed need four men to hold him down before he was taken off the island.

The two women tell how Brenda Chamberlain embraced the islanders' struggle, with Jean, Shadrach the dog, and their boat the Little Owl. *She was always willing to get involved in anything – pulling up the boat or getting in the sheep*, explained Jane Roberts. In hot weather she wore a Chinese straw hat and she regularly invited her neighbours in for tea or coffee. They regarded her as 'different', but

. . . we got used to her. She was an artist. She would take us down to the beach and show us the head of a woman in the rock. We couldn't see it, but she could. Bardsey was the happiest chapter of her life. She was never happy in Greece. She was a different Brenda. Her life was clean-cut, in blocks, different chapters. Brenda loved the island – there was an atmosphere there.

Revealingly, they suggest that it was she who introduced her superstitions to the islanders. *She wouldn't do anything on Friday 13th. I had never heard of it being bad*, said Jane Roberts.

TIDE-RACE is a collection of brilliant pictures: *silver and gold lichens enamelled a pool; hard blue mussels; soft anemones.* The descriptions are so vivid they appeal to every sense. The reader is drawn into the atmosphere of the island: its peaceful autumn days or shrouding sea fogs.

The image above is repeated (pp. 55 and 79), like others in TIDE-RACE, creating – whether deliberately or not – the effect of a pattern's motif or a poetic refrain. Brenda Chamberlain's language itself is lyrical. In its rhythms are the same traces of Celtic *oddity* found in her poetry. And there are flashes of mischievous humour, as in her tale of the island boat, which rolls *this way and that way, in transports of loneliness,* even *on a greased-pole calm.*

Her painting at this time reflects the same images as TIDE-RACE itself: rock formations worn by waves, or the strong, swarthy island people. She tells how the two forms of expression flowed together in the 1950 painting 'Children on the Seashore': the description on page 180 was written on the canvas, and the painting *blended* into the words six months later.[1] Some experts have criticized these portraits as being too *heavy* and stylized. But Rhys Gwyn in DOCK LEAVES (Autumn 1957) pointed out that the dark, unfathomable eyes gazing out passively at the harshness of the world are *the perfect reflection of her personal* Weltanschauung – *the sorrow and hopelessness felt by a sensitive person in the midst of our contemporary hell.*

Her work was her *raison d'être.* Paradoxically she regarded her *real life* as that *of the imagination.* Her own impressions were the vital raw material which fuelled her painting and writing, and without stimuli from the *outside world* she could not work. *From each new and thrilling experience the life of the imagination is reborn,* she wrote. Her island was at once a retreat and *a romance,* pricking forward her

[1] 'The Relationship between Art and Literature', NLW, MS 21501E, and a longer version in the possession of Joan Rees.

imagination to discover a new world which was, for her, real. In first crossing the Sound she begins to sense that new reality, and *to live in the present moment. For past and future merge into the living moment on and about this sea-rock.*

Enlli was the source of *a power of creative energy* and TIDE-RACE is remarkable for the sheer vigour of the world it portrays. Conran believed:

What gives TIDE-RACE its classic quality is the recalcitrance of the reality it describes: it is not content to be just the backcloth to her idealizing dream

– a dubious tribute, but making an important point. The characters have a life and complexity of their own, never becoming mere ciphers or tragic stereotypes. Cadwaladr, for instance, may be described as *the embodiment of invincible devilry*, but through the pages of the book he develops as unpredictable, courageous, proud, and yet sensitive:

. . . his savagery was shot through with tenderness of such poetry as to sometimes surprise. He could be cunningly aware of the feelings of others; he could show a grudging admiration of other men . . .

Whereas in later work, Brenda Chamberlain sometimes attempted to force her characters into the roles her imagination created for them, in TIDE-RACE she displays genuine insight into those around her. Less agonizingly *self*-conscious than in much of her work, she relates incident after incident with a generous sympathy. *Other people are necessary to us, if only to convince us of our own reality,* she wrote. On Bardsey she was most assured of that reality, bound securely into the close-knit island community with bonds she *cherished*, for her life was both happy and creative.

She discovered a bold, new relish for living; for *quaysides, foreign cities, exotic fruits.*

It remains the alighting-place of my heart, the point of seeing with a clear eye and mind . . . The life which at first seemed so confusing, so stifling, has become the releasing spring, until at last, there is no question of identity.

The book has strong currents of melancholy. The people of Bardsey, like all humanity, are puppets playing out their role in *the fatal play of life and death.* Man drives towards self-destruction. For Brenda Chamberlain, the shadow of death perpetually darkens the stage. While yearning for immortality she recognizes that

without agony, wild exaltation would also vanish . . . the force of my desire would become lost in the thought of eternity.

But TIDE-RACE is a fiercely positive work:

Who cares, who should care when a winged thistle seed drifts over the sea? There is happiness to seize, loneliness to bear.

The seed carries life forward. And *today is mine!* Life brings joy and pain, but beyond it is only *lostness . . . the cold austerity of outer regions of space.* Pity, pity the dead child Ianto

who will never sail the summer seas, nor with his father fish for fine lobster, nor know the dangers of winter in the Sound.

38

IV

Brenda Chamberlain first visited Karl von Laer in Germany at Christmas 1952. The experience made a profound emotional impact on her, and provided the inspiration for her only novel, THE WATER-CASTLE. Her first draft, the Green Note-book, date-lined London 1953 and subtitled 'The German Day-book of Elizabeth Greatorex', was eventually sold to the Welsh Arts Council in 1969 for £50 and is in the National Library of Wales; as is the hand-stitched typescript of a longer version with twenty-two letters added on. THE WATER-CASTLE was not published until 1964, and received a mixed reception.

She kept seven other German notebooks, dated 1953 to 1958, and bequeathed them in her will to Karl's son Gottfried. Although the will, made in February 1971, was invalidated by a technical error, the notebooks were sent to Germany none the less. They contain drafts for 'The Green Heart' and other published poems like 'In Old Age' and 'Bird, Flower and Vermin'.

The plot of THE WATER-CASTLE is slight: Elizabeth Greatorex visits an old friend in Germany, Klaus von Dorn, with her French husband Antoine. Klaus and Elizabeth recognize that they love each other, but Elizabeth returns home to Britain with Antoine.

Although published as a novel, it was more intimately personal than anything else Brenda

Chamberlain wrote. Elizabeth Greatorex can be closely identified with the author, Klaus with Karl von Laer, and Antoine with Jean. The Green Notebook tells how the other characters relate to Karl's family. I am convinced that these are broadly the events of that Westphalian Christmas – as Brenda Chamberlain saw them.

Numerous details link the writer and her heroine, who lives on *a half-forgotten island in the Irish Sea*. But most important is the testimony of the poems. 'The Green Heart' Parts II and III capture these experiences in almost identical words. One of many examples is found as Elizabeth's ship heads back to England: *Klaus's face was printed on the night at sea. In the long darkness, his eyes watched over me.* 'The Green Heart' Part II.vii starts:

> *Your face is printed on the night.*
> *In demon darkness of storm at sea*
> *Your eyes watch over me.*

The book further illuminates the link between the poems and Karl's letters. Elizabeth describes how she created verse from Klaus's descriptions. Arriving in Germany she recognizes the landscapes of her imagination, like the *candled fir trees* in the church on Christmas Eve, pictured in 'The Green Heart' Part I.vi. *I now so late shared his experience and found the poem true.*

In one of Klaus's paintings Elizabeth sees the *sand dunes by the Baltic. I described them to you in a letter. You wrote a poem*, Klaus tells her. The same *desert* was pictured in 'The Green Heart' Parts I.v and vi, written during the war, although Brenda Chamberlain did not see the Baltic for herself until 1958. Karl von Laer confirms how he wrote to Brenda about his 'adventure' of Christmas 1932, when he and a friend walked the sandhills between the Baltic and the Kurische Haff, to the village of Nidden.

Elizabeth even tells Klaus: *They are really your poems.* And this view is elaborated in the longer typescript of THE WATER-CASTLE, in which Elizabeth tells of the poems she wrote about the departure of her friend (here called Franz) from London in 1933 [*sic*]; the journey that took him to the city of Amsterdam:

I have been writing poems for him, as his double, all these years. They have been written either as if from his heart and mind or have been a fusion of his and mine, inextricably entwined.

Karl von Laer's letters confirm the merging of fact and fiction. Numerous events from the book are found in them. Elizabeth describes Selma's drawing of the game 'Six Six Quick Quick' on a chocolate wrapper (p. 94) and Klaus's letter from Goslar with its phantom trees (p. 106). Identical documents are in the National Library of Wales. (Selma represents Karl's friend Ulla Kruger.) Words used by Klaus (p. 80) come from Karl's letter of February 1953. Furthermore the formal, poetic phrases in which Klaus and Elizabeth acknowledge their love for each other, forming the climax of the novel (pp. 128–30), are taken almost entirely from that same letter (which featured too in 'The Green Heart').

What was this strange and intense relationship, and why did the two of them remain separated throughout their lives? After the war Brenda Chamberlain was divorced, and Karl von Laer remarried twice. In 'I think of you in a time of storm'[1] she wrote: *Can you reach my side / To make me your bride.* Yet could she have been happy with the prosaic reality of marriage?

In the typescript of THE WATER-CASTLE Elizabeth describes the day in 1932 when she first noticed *passion* on the young German's face, and adds *Why I had not fallen in love with the ardent boy, I do not know.* In her early poems there was *no hint of passion,* only *an idealised romantic love.* It was Brenda Chamberlain's reunion with von Laer which seems to have given the relationship a new significance.

She was convinced that Jean was consumed with the jealousy attributed to Antoine in THE WATER-CASTLE. Karl referred to her anxiety about it in several letters in 1953, and advised her to stay with Jean, telling her she would be unhappy without him. After their fateful visit, Karl wrote to Jean in German regretting that they had quarrelled because of him, and assuring the Frenchman that he did not intend to take Brenda away from him. Karl did indeed believe, as in Elizabeth's prologue, that the excitement of the trip had thrown *too much sunshine* on Brenda Chamberlain's heart; and that her imagination had exaggerated their relationship, encouraged by the distance between them.

Several friends have suggested that Brenda Chamberlain drew back from physical love. And in

[1] LIFE AND LETTERS, June 1950; also in *Botteghe Oscure*, v, 1950 as 'Song of a woman from the Western Island'. A version of 'The Green Heart' III.iii.

the typescript introduction, writing *about* Elizabeth Greatorex and not through her, the writer describes the German again as *her 'double' – (he could scarcely be called her lover)*. As good friends they would be closer than husband and wife, declared von Laer. *Your friendship is more than anything else in the world. For friendship, you must be close in the souls,* he wrote in March 1953. For years, Brenda Chamberlain's romantic passion flowed into this spiritual communion.

The closeness of the author and her material flaws THE WATER-CASTLE as a novel. The qualities which made her so successful as a journal writer prevented her achieving the degree of objectivity necessary to the novelist. Reviewers complained that THE WATER-CASTLE lacked plot or structure; that it was too *sentimental*; and that the author was not *standing at the right distance from her canvas*.

The trouble about the book is less that it is slight – that was never any hindrance to being memorable – but that it is rather tediously adolescent in its solemnity and its endless and inconclusive analysis of mood.
(THE TIMES LITERARY SUPPLEMENT, 13 February 1964)

THE SPECTATOR (14 February 1964) found a *serious technical fault* in the book and highlighted the *gap . . . between what has been observed and what seems to have been invented.*

Elizabeth describes the main characters: Antoine, Klaus and his wife Helga, in subjective, one-dimensional terms, offering little evidence for the feelings she ascribes to them. Indeed, sometimes events seem to contradict her conclusions. Her dramatic statements are expressed in strong, emotive vocabulary. But these characters do not develop convincingly. It is the minor figures, with whom she is less emotionally involved, who stand out as real people: Kurt and Selma Hastfer, still full of vigour despite their wartime trauma; and the children, timid and excitable. Through these and many others, Brenda Chamberlain builds up a portrait of post-war Europe with its tribes of refugees, deprived of their gracious life-style by a cataclysmic upheaval and striving defiantly to revive the grandeur of the past at the crowded Obernberg, through hare shoots and lavish entertainment.

An atmosphere of tension, of growing crisis, is built up through a succession of minor incidents – incidents which Elizabeth loads with significance. The two potted cyclamen Klaus gives to the women, for instance, become potent symbols of their rivalry. The tone is naïve, earnest, and gravely portentous – hardly justified by the predictable denouement. This suggestive quality sometimes adds up to an indulgent vagueness reminiscent of 'The Green Heart'.

It is interesting that there are three quotations from Rilke in THE WATER-CASTLE, for Kenneth Rexroth deprecated his influence on British writers in the 1940s, claiming that translations by Spender and Leishman made Rilke's precise vocabulary and imagery become imprecise and *moody*. There is no doubt that Chamberlain was deeply influenced by Rilke. It was Alun Lewis who recommended his work to her *as a rich source of words for the same fundamental thoughts as you work in*. Translations of his poems are among her papers in the National Library of Wales, and she highlighted Lewis's own devotion to *the mystic* in a posthumous review in THE DUBLIN MAGAZINE (October–December 1945).

In Germany that winter she visited an old friend of Rilke and his wife Clara, Frau Hertha Koenig, and according to her notebooks was deeply moved by the encounter. Frau Koenig showed her handwritten poems and photographs of the poet which *showed him sitting full face, his large, deep-set eyes gazing with melancholy at the world.* How remarkably this description resembles Brenda Chamberlain's contemporary portraits, and that same *Weltanschauung* they express. She later wrote a poem about this experience, 'At Mrs King's Water-Castle' (Koenig being German for King), and in her notes identified Rilke as the *poet* referred to.

Another link is that the names *Brita, Sophie, Vivika* and *Hastfer*, used in THE WATER-CASTLE, all appear in one of Rilke's letters in the same collection as Brenda Chamberlain's Foreword:

Everything that befalls us is of one piece, in whose correlations one thing is kith and kin with another, fashions its own birth, grows and is educated to its own needs, and we have ultimately only to be there, simply, fervently, as the earth is there, in harmony with the seasons . . .

(from a letter to Clara Rilke,
SELECTED LETTERS OF RAINER MARIA RILKE, 1946)

For Elizabeth the correlations, the pattern, are clear:

I began to trace my life back over the years to the first days with Klaus. How could I not have realised until this night on a storm-tossed ship that I had, as a girl of 20, given my soul for ever into his keeping?

In this brief period she perceives life with a unique intensity: *It seems likely to remain the most real part of my whole life.* Equally Germany, like Bardsey, offered Brenda Chamberlain a new stimulus. *In such a new and thrilling encounter the life of the imagination is reborn,* says Elizabeth, echoing the words of Tide-Race.

The writer sees and evokes the world around her with perceptive accuracy, creating vivid images and building up, through the winter scenery and the sense of nostalgia, a gripping atmosphere of melancholy:

Scarcely a gleam of sun has pierced the snow clouds since our arrival. We ask, does the sun never shine here? There has been a gently persistent snowfall every day this week. White clouds like a giant's breath, black clouds like a pestilence, descend.

Sharp little pictures – a village crib or nurses walking in the snow – interrupt the narrative as they are observed. For Chamberlain followed Gide's maxim: *It is a mistake to intend to write only very important things in a journal. That is not its justification* ('A Total Eclipse of the Sun', Mabon, Spring 1972).

Elizabeth's imagination works at fever pitch throughout her stay, so that although she may believe her experience to be 'real', it begins – like the trees on the Rehberg that are fashioned by the mist into fabulous beasts – to resemble the stuff of fairy tales. *Each of us inhabits his own world and all our worlds are unreal,* she confesses.

Everything must conform to the picture built up in her imagination by Klaus's letters. Instead of allowing the unity of experience to develop according to *its own needs,* as Rilke counselled, Elizabeth attempts

46

to impose her own pattern. The critic's epithet of *adolescent* is applicable, for she has a naïve and romantic belief that life will not rebel against her expectations, or the pattern be spoilt:

I cannot believe she [Helga] *will ever be the mistress of Schlotheim . . . it is for me to go. Schlotheim is part of my myth-inheritance.*

It is quite possible for a novel written in the first person to demonstrate that the narrator is under false apprehensions. It can even be achieved by the novelist unconsciously, without damaging the work. In THE WATER-CASTLE, however, it is an unintentional weakness, stemming from Brenda Chamberlain's identification with Elizabeth and her desire to convey her own intensely personal experience. The book might even be seen as her bid to come to terms with her fierce and complex emotion.

Her attempt to turn it into a novel undermines its force. The novelist generally creates a world that – though it may be imaginary – tells us about the world we live in.

As Conran pointed out, Brenda Chamberlain was

a novelist in reverse: for the novelist believes himself real and invents out of his experience an imaginary world for our edification and delight. Brenda Chamberlain's great act of fiction was herself, steering her imagination between the real islands of a real outside.

Elizabeth Greatorex represented her image of herself in her imagination.

Writing of Brenda Chamberlain's art, Rhys Gwyn

described it as Expressionistic: *basically motivated by psychological forces*, by an *inner need*. But he warned that it should still *express* rather than *depict* emotion. *When this essential distinction becomes blurred the result is egocentricity.* In her writing, too, Brenda Chamberlain sometimes fell prey to the temptation to describe rather than enact her theme, to use it for *the depiction of her own mood*, resulting in a self-indulgence which threatened the quality of her work. This *lack of subtlety* in her subjects arose not from a shortage of perception on her part, but a desire to put across her own – Brenda Chamberlain's – vision. Life, however, is complex, paradoxical, even messy. Attempts to reorder this complexity lead to stylization, deadening, for which any formal pattern, however exquisite, is a poor substitute.

THE WATER-CASTLE is not among Brenda Chamberlain's best work, even though some reviewers called it *superlative* (AUCKLAND WEEKLY NEWS, 13 May 1964) and *a remarkable first novel* (PUNCH, 19 February 1964). BOOKS OF THE MONTH was more accurate in finding in it

a definite flavour of its own: the book has a marked quality of indirect statement so that what is said lingers in the mind and often has a kind of delayed impact.

Indeed it is a haunting work that lingers and reverberates in the consciousness. It is pervaded by a melancholy fatalism, full of forebodings about the future of Europe and humanity. Little sense of hope or renewal breaks through this barren pessimism. Yet it is a book of extraordinary intensity, embodying one of the most striking and persistent motifs in the pattern of Brenda Chamberlain's life.

V

Brenda Chamberlain was over fifty when she left Wales, alone, to make her home on the island of Ydra (*Hydra*). She was drawn spellbound to Greece, land of her *spiritual birth*, by a *dream of classical myth*. She found the modern country disconcertingly foreign, more like the East than the cradle of Western civilization. Yet her third book of prose, A ROPE OF VINES, is imbued with the classical Greek fatalism noted in her earlier work; as if, having been led to the home of those powers she always superstitiously acknowledged, she became enthralled by them:

Are we, because we live in the classical context of Greece, simply puppets hounded and bewildered by the Furies?

When she first visited Greece in 1962 Brenda Chamberlain was already *haunted* by the theme of a book: *it had to be set on a Greek island, in a peasant community* (ARTISTS IN WALES). A ROPE OF VINES was published three years later. Again it drew on her notebooks, written in Ydra between May 1963 and May 1964. Embryonic elements are found in a piece of autobiographical prose about her first visit, dated September–October 1962, owned by Joan Rees; and a shorter version in the National Library of Wales, published as 'Abstract of a Journal 1962' (MABON, Summer 1970).

The book's publishers, Hodder and Stoughton, compared A ROPE OF VINES to Virginia Woolf's journals. Yet they expressed some misgivings about how the *smarty boots on the Sunday papers* would respond to the author's strong sensibility.[1] To some extent they were justified in fearing this quality to be out of fashion. Yet generally the critics' response, although more limited than to TIDE-RACE, was favourable.

Comparisons were inevitably drawn with TIDE-RACE, and indeed there are many similarities. Both books share a journal format. Here the narrator is still more closely identified with the writer, for she is addressed as 'Brenda' by the characters. In both books she is essaying life on a small, fairly remote and barren island, where the rigours of survival leave the inhabitants tenaciously independent and richly idiosyncratic.

Another common feature is the influence of the sea:

I find myself surprised by homesickness for my own island when small fishing-boats come into sight, with men standing up in them, as they do in the Enlli craft.

Here, the women light fragrant candles in the *monasteri* as they wait helplessly for their seamen husbands' return. These *fire-gleaming, passionate waters* also batter the bodies of half-drowned islanders – a brutal reminder of the nearness of death. In times of stress, the sea provided Brenda Chamberlain's *measure of strength*, as if she were unable to live where she could not look out on it and find in its beauty and awesomeness the essence of

---

[1] From a letter in the possession of Joan Rees.

life itself. *There need only be a glimpse of salt water . . .*
and I am myself again.

THE SUNDAY TIMES echoed previous reviews in
describing A ROPE OF VINES as *a painter's writing,*
sharp with visual imagery. The atmosphere of the
island is powerfully conveyed: a harsh, abrasive
world that has *lost its eyebrows,* burnt by

a ferocious heat: the slopes of grey rock and whitened herbs in
certain places taking the full sun seemed to be lit with thick
flames, the air was filled with the smell of scorching.

Once more, her economical use of words and lyrical
style combine to create *a series of prose poems, evocative*
through sight, smell and sound (THE SUNDAY TIMES, 29
August 1965).

On Ydra, Brenda Chamberlain's imagination works
as powerfully as ever, peopling the island with
figures from legend and history. As in TIDE-RACE she
is acutely aware both of the supernatural and the
past. She finds Ydra an *uneasy island, ghost-ridden,*
and with black danger in the air. The narrator and her
friend Leonidas share a psychic apprehension both
of one another and of their surroundings. He is
agonized to fever pitch by the *expectation of*
earthquake; while she, after his departure, is shaken
by the potent presence of his ghost.

During her brief retreat to the Orthodox nunnery of
Agios Efpraxia, she feels *the old gods are almost if not*
quite dead. Yet the assurance is short-lived. Lighting
candles before the Virgin or praying with the nuns, she
yearns for a reassuring orthodoxy; *a belief in something*
beyond myself, call it God, the Cross, the Ever-Virgin.

Her friend Esme Kirby confirms that Brenda Chamberlain was tempted at one time to adopt the Catholic faith. Here, conviction escapes her, and she is drawn back to *the inimical forces* – the Fates:

Since childhood I have believed in the mask, the blood upon the steps, the chorus saying this is inevitable, these things are because they must be.

Indeed, when she lights a candle in the *monasteri* it is not to appease a beneficent God, but to *tempt the wind, to take a gambler's chance of its being blown out or surviving, as a gauge to the day's fortune. This world is still pagan and rooted in superstition.* In their own land, the capricious deities of Greek mythology dictate the inexorable destinies of their subjects.

Brenda Chamberlain draws on this ancient culture, rather than any accurate knowledge of the customs and beliefs of the modern Greeks, as her background. As ever, her own perceptions are what interest her, and the glimpses of universal truth she gleans from them.

She remained an outsider among the Ydriots, so it is more contrived when she ascribes to the Greek islanders the same recognition of the tragic condition of their lives as that attributed to their Celtic counterparts. It is expressed instinctively by Aldo's mother:

. . . singing into a black night and a heaven of stars her grief and despair, strong and inevitable as the fall of waves against the land; a primitive, lost cry of the heart of a savage woman in a poor cottage lost on a Greek island.

Like the Enlli folk, these Greeks are tough, passionate and generous. From her window the writer attentively observes their harsh, dramatic lives: the women beating leaves from the trees to feed their goats, or herding a young truant back to school; the funeral of an old woman, or a fight at Loulou's taverna. Brenda Chamberlain revels in the melodrama of the quarrels and triumphs which *enliven* the villagers, lifting them above the soul-destroying daily routine. She succeeds again in bringing these minor characters to life: Twitch-Sophia and her crabby mother who screech at one another into the night; Aldo the boy who bites; and Elene's husband dancing arrogantly in his spiv's black and white winkle-picker shoes.

Kyffin Williams suggested that Brenda Chamberlain's *intense sensitivity* and *romanticism* led her to seek the *security of islands, where, cut off from the real world, she could indulge in her own world of fantasy.* There is much truth in this, although she was never really 'cut off'. The islands were like miniature worlds where she could more readily find a clear identity:

For some years, I have been on the fringe of other people's lives. Now, on this island, I have found my way of life again, having my own table at Graphos', with my friends, my guests,

she declares. Yet she could not fulfil the same active role in the community that she established on Ynys Enlli.

Ydra is depicted as a brutal environment,

an island of terror, where no gentleness is, no cool glades in which to hide oneself away while wounds grow shining new skin.

But the writer's suffering is spiritual rather than physical, for she commits herself to the experience with characteristic fervour. Her heart is anchored to the island, just as the boats of the Ydriot seamen of old were held by cables of vine tendrils.

Brenda Chamberlain made her home on Ydra in search of a new creative stimulus, another *romance . . . full of gypsy-colour and excitement*. She put her faith, she affirmed, in *the irrational*; and throughout her life acted impulsively from her desire for love, for happiness and for new sensations. Yet at the same time she was beguiled by a vision of *voluntary imprisonment* in a world of moral and aesthetic purity and natural beauty; a contemplative life safe from emotional upheaval.

In A ROPE OF VINES this conflict is crystallized in the narrator's withdrawal to the nunnery. *Solitude is necessary to me, so that I can hear the earth breathing. The voices of men and women dement me after a time*, she declares. Arriving on Ydra, she is attracted at once to the hilltop monasteries. But once among the nuns of Agios Efpraxia, it is their unrepentant womanliness she cherishes most, symbolized by their surprising violet underwear.

As on Bardsey, seclusion increases the writer's appetite for life. She becomes restless and rebellious, and from the security of the *monasteri* looks down with longing on the dangerous excitement of the town below, like a *gargoyle in a corner of the terrace, leaning out over the world*. Although Brenda Chamberlain never determined *once and for all, this I want, that I reject*, her clear view from the mountain-top refuge leads her to conclude: *though only half-willing to leave this high situation, I am for the battle of the market-place*.

Her dilemma was highlighted in reviews which appeared in September and October 1965. Alec Reid in the GUARDIAN called the book a *compelling blow-by-blow account* of the writer's *richly creative personal conflict*. The BOOK EXAMINER agreed that *she emerges with new understanding of herself and human existence*. And Norman Thomas, in BOOKS AND BOOKMEN, believed Brenda Chamberlain was undergoing a period of personal crisis. A ROPE OF VINES is a more intimate and more introspective work that TIDE-RACE, for she confesses: *It is time for a stocktaking of the spirit*. THE SCOTSMAN felt she was writing for herself, *so that to read is to be caught looking impertinently over her shoulder*.

This earnestness did not find favour everywhere. *She moves in on one too fast, and too insistently*, complained the IRISH TIMES. The TIMES LITERARY SUPPLEMENT protested:

Miss Chamberlain's heart is always wide open, and every emotional chord she touches tends to be played fortissimo, so that a curious atmosphere of falsity and exaggeration hangs over even her most insightful passages.

The emotional tension reaches a peak after Leonidas is arrested for accidentally killing an Englishman. The narrator is beset by *insane pressures:*

How far can I bend before I break, how much salt water cover my head before I drown?

There is an atmosphere of sustained crisis and growing panic. How aptly she writes of her *astonished nerves*, for every encounter startles her raw sensitivity.

More self-conscious and less assured of her *own* reality than in TIDE-RACE, Brenda Chamberlain in this book sometimes loses what Conran calls *a three-dimensional sense of other people's viewpoints.* Whereas on Bardsey she knew she was part of other people's lives, here the gypsies in the mountains exist for her, but not she for them. Consequently the main characters, as in THE WATER-CASTLE, remain vague, unconvincing figures acting out the roles imposed on them. Leonidas, in particular, is a Greek hero in the ancient mould, a victim of the Fates, led on by an arbitrary but immutable destiny.

It is impossible to say how much of A ROPE OF VINES refers to 'real' events, for the conventional boundaries of reality and imagination are blurred, especially after the shock of Leonidas's arrest. The tone changes to take on a new intensity. Time loses its continuity. Reality becomes subject to the crazy logic of dreams, while nightmares and fantasies are as vivid as *life as it is called.* As her imagination runs out of control the narrator loses certainty even of her own substance:

Who is this woman I stare at in the mirror? Did I invent her, or did she make me up in the glass?

And Leonidas, have I invented him too, because he was necessary to me?

How can anybody be sure what reality is? How can we know when truth is being evaded, if an idea is fantastic, or if it is born of a deeper perception than ours? Captain Theophanis paces the port thinking of *phantom liners* he has sailed.

It is possible to live a lie until it is a kind of truth, until a beauty comes out of even so timid a pretence.

Brenda Chamberlain's perplexity about the essence of reality was never resolved. She was not unaware, as A ROPE OF VINES suggests, of her tendency to escape into fantasy. In ALUN LEWIS AND THE MAKING OF THE CASEG BROADSHEETS she wrote of the need to keep *a balance between dream and reality* when living alone in the mountains. In the catalogue for her 1963 Arts Council exhibition, 'Two Painters', she made this analysis:

A work of art is a mystery that springs partly from nature and partly from the inner world of the artist. This inner world is a private place inhabited by the artist during the greater part of his life. The nature of the vie intérieure *varies from artist to artist; in one case, it may be . . . a world of dream or myth or phantasy* [sic]. *In another, it is a world rooted in reality, but following a private pattern, an individual idiom.*

In her later writing she became increasingly introverted, and acknowledged that her work was difficult to understand; even though Rhys Gwyn had warned against artistic *egocentricity*, since it negates the essential *communication between artist and spectator*, which *must be bilateral if it is to succeed*. If a work of art does not find recognition in the hearts and imagination of others – however much effort that recognition demands – it has failed.

D. H. Lawrence wrote that:

The essential quality of poetry is that it makes a new effort of attention, and 'discovers' a new world within the known world.
(PHOENIX, Heinemann, 1936)

This applies just as well to prose. The artist tears through the *umbrella*, the *painted vault* under which

Lawrence pictured humanity sheltering; to *discover* the *surging chaos* beyond, and extend our ways of seeing. But no matter how startling the vision, it reaches out to a world that is 'real'; to *nature*. Brenda Chamberlain was capable of that *effort of attention*. She was, in the words of Jonah Jones, *a quiet spoken visionary*.

In A ROPE OF VINES, in contrast to Elizabeth's assertion in THE WATER-CASTLE, the writer concludes: *We invent our own lives, but there remains reality outside oneself.* She explains:

It is comparatively easy to endure the searing ecstasy of the rarefied peaks, very hard to accept the small pricks of daily life.

It was this latter definition of reality: mediocre, *boring in its repetitions*, to which Brenda Chamberlain could not resign herself. Like the 'Dead Climber' she strove to transcend the *endless night of the valley*.

Monotony, time's relentless passage, was her enemy; like the grandfather clock in her Bardsey home, *telling me that death runs at my heels*. In A ROPE OF VINES she highlights the need to overcome *the fear of growing old, of the years that press us down towards the grave*, for that fear paralyses us. Those who fear death fear life as well, for death is always present. Frightened to meet any challenge, they lead a *machine-driven existence of Sunday-dinner futility*, and deny responsibility for their own lives.

Often we try to distort time, to control it to suit our own needs. But that is impossible. Only those – like the *lusty people of the wells* of Kala Pigadhia – who accept the rhythm of time and come to terms with death as part of its cycle, *know a meaningful pattern of*

behaviour ordered by the nature of their surroundings.
They are like the dancers in T. S. Eliot's FOUR
QUARTETS (echoed repeatedly in her work):

> *Keeping time,*
> *Keeping the rhythm in their dancing*
> *As in their living in the living seasons*

In a 1933 letter in the typescript of THE WATER-
CASTLE, quoted also in the published version (p. 100),
'Franz' urged Elizabeth: *Do not see the minutes and*
hours on the watch, the days and years on the calendar.
They do not matter. He continued:

One moment, one creative moment is better than a hundred
days when you go through the world like a mouldy-warp, eating
and sleeping.

It was a philosophy Brenda Chamberlain took to her
heart, aspiring always to the timeless, *living moment,*
the moment of intensity and illumination – like
Eliot's moment in the rose-garden – to which she
responded with the full scope of her emotions. In A
ROPE OF VINES she acknowledges that moments of
suffering are also timeless, giving us an instant of
clear vision; putting life in perspective. These
apprehensions must be remembered and
understood, not hastily forgotten in a bid to avoid
the pain. *To learn to be wiser through suffering, that is*
the kernel. Brenda Chamberlain believed in *creative, as*
opposed to material, reality . . . Reality that touches the
nerves and heart (review of HA! HA! AMONG THE
TRUMPETS, THE DUBLIN MAGAZINE, October 1945).

She is conscious here of the constraints of mortality:
to be alive is to be trapped within the flesh, within the

mind, within the pattern of days and nights. Yet A ROPE OF VINES shares the same courageous love of life as TIDE-RACE. It invites us to challenge fate, to be prepared to risk suffering and failure, to take responsibility; for life takes on the meaning we give it. *Isn't the secret of living, to be committed to someone, to something?*

The narrator chooses to commit herself to Leonidas, despite the pain this brings. For she concludes that mutual dependence on other living beings is the fulfilment of human life, summed up by Dostoyevsky: *For a woman, all resurrection, all salvation, from whatever perdition, lies in love.*

The Foreword of A ROPE OF VINES expresses this commitment in practice. It is taken from Thomas Mann's THE HOLY SINNER, the story of Grigorss, who achieves righteousness through the severest isolation and self-denial. Drawn as she was to a monastic life, Brenda Chamberlain believed even more strongly that once the human spirit is cut off from others, *the animal takes over.* The Tibetan Yetis which the Greek Yanis's friend claims are the descendants of holy men, call to mind Wolfgang, the hermit of TIDE-RACE, whose solitary search for God led him instead to the devil within himself. *Without the help of man he could not hope to find God.* The words Chamberlain takes from Mann are not of Grigorss himself, but the woman who sinfully loves him:

I would share his suffering with him without his knowledge, in order perhaps to be his good angel.

The sea is the symbol of this affirmation. *I am for ocean, the tumult of thalassa,* declares the writer. In its *light-filled depths* are all manner of secrets, to be discovered by the 'heroes' who dare to venture forth. *O sailors, O voyagers* she greets them, echoing Eliot's words: *O voyagers, O seamen.* Thus the sea offers progress towards understanding, the fruitful use of time, just as for Eliot it represents time eternal. Men must be explorers and *fare forward* over the *vast waters / Of the petrel and the porpoise* towards the unknown.

A ROPE OF VINES recognizes that the material conditions of life cannot be escaped, but that raw matter can be transformed, enlivened: *The earth has need of the energy of man's nostrils.* In responding *fervently* and fitly to every experience, we may aspire to a different 'reality'.

It is the sea which once more supplies Brenda Chamberlain's image: the caiques prove their material substance by *grinding their bows against the stubborn rocks of the quayside.* But they are transformed:

. . . why should not the squat wooden hulks with swaying masts that rise questing into the darkness speak for me, for mankind, for the sieved seas and the thymy mountains. They join the sky to the earth by stretching their yards heavenward.

The human imagination takes in and transforms the 'given' in attaining knowledge and understanding:

the black sky is grasped at . . . a god is being invoked. The tall masts sprout green leaves. The god and the identifying vessels fuse.

VI

THE PROTAGONISTS and POEMS WITH DRAWINGS were both completed in the late 1960s, and share a growing sense of loss and desperation.

> *Love and embrace the dwellers in remote gardens,*
> *who know the south wind of springtime, the*
> *south wind of desire . . .*

> *How hard to remember an olive tree when the*
> *soul is behind bars.*
> (THE PROTAGONISTS and POEMS WITH DRAWINGS)

Both drew on Brenda Chamberlain's experiences in Greece.

THE PROTAGONISTS was written in October to November 1967, six months after the Greek military take-over. In an interview with Alan McPherson in FORECAST, the University College of North Wales newspaper, in April 1968, she told of its composition. She never planned to write a play, although she was thinking, before the coup, of a film she would like to make about Greece. She started it after a trip to the prison island of Leros, and continued after a second visit. But she did not see it as drama until she showed it to an American friend who responded: *My God, how strong, this is a play!* After that she sat down to write at eight o'clock every morning *as though a key had been turned on something, it came so fast.* She took her notebook to the port to record *direct speech.*

*It just happened through their voices, it was terribly
exciting.*

She kept the work a secret in Greece, and when
friends advised her not to talk about Leros she joked:
Well, I'll just say there were lovely flowers there. She did
not want to involve the Greek peasant family she
was living with. So on completion, THE PROTAGON-
ISTS was read by six *trusted* friends, and then
smuggled out of the country. Back in Britain, Brenda
Chamberlain offered the play to various organiza-
tions. It was sent to the Royal Shakespeare Company
and read by the Literary Adviser Jeremy Brooks who
responded enthusiastically:

I've just finished reading THE PROTAGONISTS, *and want to
write at once and tell you that I think it is a most distinguished
and powerful piece of writing. I don't quite know why it is so
compelling to read, since so many of its effects are virtually
subliminal, but I do know that I did not want to stop reading
and that I laid it down with that feeling of satisfaction one gets
after encountering a fully-achieved work of art.*[1]

Yet he also recorded reservations about its production:

*Whether it is a play or not I don't yet know. You make your
dramas more by a pattern of ideas than by a progression of
actions and the question must be whether that pattern is strong
enough to withstand the strain and degree of loss that go with
public performance.*

[1] From a letter, 17 April 1968, in the possession of Joan
Rees. Extracts are found in a letter from Brenda Chamber-
lain to Meic Stephens, 26 April 1968, in NLW; and in the
Welsh Drama Studio's programme.

He compared its *fusion of elements* to the work of David Jones, and promised to show it to the RSC's Artistic Director, Trevor Nunn. Brenda Chamberlain was thrilled by his *immediate and wonderful response.*

In the event THE PROTAGONISTS was performed at the Pritchard Jones Hall of the University College, Bangor, on 11 and 12 October 1968, by the Welsh Drama Studio, a semi-professional company newly formed by David Lyn to be a *comprehensively Welsh theatre group* (NORTH WALES CHRONICLE, 26 September 1968). David Lyn, an actor whose career spanned the Royal Shakespeare Company, the Welsh Theatre Company and the BBC, was looking for new plays by Welsh authors to launch a *renaissance* in Bangor. The Welsh Drama Studio was heralded as the *natural expression of the culture of the people.* The production was sponsored by the North Wales Association for the Arts, and rehearsed that summer under Brenda Chamberlain's supervision *in all sorts of places in Bangor from a cellar to the university* (Alan Twelves, NORTH WALES CHRONICLE, 1 August 1968). *My respect for it grew as we worked into the production,* recalls David Lyn.

Most of the players were local people, but the leading female role, L, was taken by Sophia Michopoulou, a Greek professional and for eight years a member of the Carolus Coun Company in Athens, who came to Wales especially for the production. THE PROTAGONISTS has not been performed since then, and although Hodder and Stoughton helped with retyping, the play was never published. Extracts, taken from a 1966 journal, appeared posthumously in MABON (Spring 1972). Others were adapted as poems for POETRY WALES

(Spring 1970), the Welsh Arts Council 1970 'Word and Image' exhibition, and 'Dial-a-poem' (1971).

The play has little plot and not much action. It is built round the interaction of the eight characters: six prisoners distinguished only by letters, a Guard and an Edict-maker. The characters (apart from Z and L) lack individual identity. They are mere 'protagonists' – humanity; casting doubt on Brenda Chamberlain's claim that as she wrote she found they were *always themselves*. David Lyn actually transferred speeches from one to another. As the play develops, the roles are reversed, demonstrating the central theme that we all share the same human weaknesses. Once in possession of power, the prisoners are just as capable of cruelty and arrogance as their former masters.

THE PROTAGONISTS examines the *universality of the nature of power, tyranny and corruption*. Yet Brenda Chamberlain correctly denied making political propaganda. *It was simply the result of enormous pressure and misery and being absolutely unable to do a thing*, she declared. It was her own personal, *emotional reaction* to the shock of military dictatorship, to loud-speakers in the squares, police surveillance, curfews, and the *uncanny total negativeness.* She wrote it to compensate for not *taking to the hills*.

She wanted the audience to experience her own sense of horror. So the play was performed almost 'in the round', with the public on three sides, the stage on the fourth, and acting areas on different levels in the middle. On the stage were scaffolding cages, against a dark backcloth. The stark setting was to encourage the spectators to use their imaginations to transform the auditorium into *Leros or any arid island.* The action should be as close to them as possible: *in and around and among them.*

Although Chamberlain recognized that the theatre makes its impact *by artifice,* using *subtle, insidious* means, the play sets out openly to intimidate and incriminate the audience, shifting guilt from the characters on the stage to the observers – us – anyone who in smug complacency shrugs off the suffering of others. David Lyn was sceptical of whether this aggressive approach would achieve its aim, and persuaded her to make some changes, omitting lengthy passages bombarding the audience with 'edicts'. Those who saw or took part in the performance stressed the powerful atmosphere created. Although the sense of the words is often unclear, they build up to an emotional fever pitch.

Of the two characters who stand out, Z is patently mad, in a play where the dividing line between madness and sanity is finely drawn. His characteristics are derived from Wolfgang, Bardsey's devil-ridden Polish hermit. The division of his body between God and the devil, the gabbled words of the Mass, the soldier who tickled his throat with a breadknife and the offer of soup; all tie in with the figure in TIDE-RACE. L on the other hand is the only woman in the play, and it is she who expresses words of hope and compassion. A number of her speeches were published as poems, suggesting that Brenda Chamberlain identified herself with the character; writing herself into her drama, just as into her prose, even if here the context is not obviously autobiographical. L's faith in regeneration can be seen as characteristic of a woman's approach to life, in contrast to the destructive anger of the male personae around her.

Yet in her writing Brenda Chamberlain did not identify herself clearly with either sex, although the leading characters around her were always men. As in THE WATER-CASTLE, she tended to show little sympathy for other women who rivalled her own unconscious pre-eminence. In life, too, despite a few close and long-standing female friends, her actions were most often influenced by her feelings for one man or another. Throughout her life she entered into a series of intense relationships – artistic and personal – with different men, some considerably younger than her. They may have regarded her as fascinating and attractive; yet none of these liaisons gave her lasting happiness. In Chamberlain's account of her first trip to Greece in 1962 (Joan Rees's copy), a significant sentence has been crossed out: *A journey should only be undertaken with the right man, where is the right man?* Esme Kirby believed that Brenda Chamberlain *desperately wanted to be loved*, and suggested that her final despair may have been induced partly by realizing that the devotion she lavished on the individuals she loved was not fully reciprocated.

L's vision of the *dwellers in remote gardens* is a hymn to freedom, a full and sensual appreciation of life. But here these values are crushed by another, darker side of Chamberlain's vision. For THE PROTAGONISTS is a desolate and pessimistic work. The prison bars which loom over the stage symbolize the isolation of every one of us. Too frightened to commit ourselves to one another, we fail to recognize our mutual dependence, and wound each other in a frantic bid for personal survival. The prisoners blame their guards for their suffering, but the Guard himself is just as much a captive. Life itself becomes a cage:

H: *You out there, how does it feel?*

J: *Much the same as inside. I can still see bars in front of my face.*

Yet total freedom is too frightening, involving as it does total responsibility. So society surrounds itself with rules and restrictions which divide and destroy people.

It is *when the soul is behind bars* that we lose our humanity. L is liberated by her faith, her imagination, for *Faith is half the cure.* The power of the imagination is immense. Z, for instance, is most dangerous to the tyrants *because he sees sparrows as eagles, and can convince you that he has seen them.* Yet more often in this play the imagination is used for escape. When J says, *To keep sane, we have to invent our own lives,* it is not acknowledging reality outside, but shutting it out. Imagination is dedicated to *forgetfulness* or nostalgia. For a *sense of reality* brings too much suffering. Z's imagination is as powerful as reality itself. Yet he is mad. Is this the inevitable result of a particularly strong sensitivity? The artist, Brenda Chamberlain implies, is close to madness and at the end of her life she was exploring the theme of insanity in her work. (See her account of being in hospital, NLW, MS 21501E.) In THE PROTAGONISTS the defiance found in much of her other work has disappeared. It is a play of unfulfilled hopes – friends who never turned up – and betrayal. Suffering is piled on suffering till the senses are numb.

Violence is everywhere: violent assault on bodies and minds, screaming, insults and obscenities. Ideas tumble out, but often they are incoherent and contradictory. J's assertion that the dead *have the advantage over us. They are quiet,* rings with despair and resignation. A repellent description of brains being voluntarily blown out and a sick pun which transforms *family size* into *suisize* foreshadow Brenda Chamberlain's own death within four years of writing this play. There is no *clinic against mortality.* Human life is lived in the shadow of death, unreconciled, for *age brings no wisdom.* In the end people, blindly *determined to survive* at the expense of others, run like the rats who plague the scene into a bestial annihilation. We are left at the end to contemplate *the death in all of us.*

THE PROTAGONISTS is an inaccessible work, confirming Kyffin Williams's view that Brenda Chamberlain retreated deeper and deeper into her own private world. Furthermore, if she had difficulty achieving the degree of 'enactment' necessary for a novel, she was even less at home with the constraints of the drama format.

In FORECAST, a Marxist reviewer denied that the play could be an *expression of solidarity with the people of Greece* if it did not see events in political terms. The critic found the work *rich in poetic and dramatic inventiveness,* but *self-indulgent,* and incoherent. The prisoners are *a bunch of ideologically bankrupt liberal intellectuals who are motivated only by nostalgia.* Their only salvation is in *lonely lyricism.* Its attempts to make oppression, imprisonment and death in a foreign country real to a middle-aged, middle-class audience create an atmosphere of *sustained hysteria,* judged FORECAST.

The analysis is in some respects perceptive, but fails to recognize that Brenda Chamberlain eschewed political ideologies, preferring to examine how *individuals* react, what they *do, feel and think* under such stress. In THE PROTAGONISTS, however, her faith in this pure individualism began to falter.

In her youth, Brenda Chamberlain regarded the artist as a superior being, set apart from the rest of humanity. This was one source of her artistic *egocentricity*, for if her own perceptions stemmed from a unique sensitivity, how could the mediocre masses hope to comprehend them? Alun Lewis urged her to bring her art out into *the streets where also there is much danger and fortitude*. Her later work showed the beginning of that move into society. Her experience in Greece awakened rudimentary political allegiances – evident also in A ROPE OF VINES – as she recognized that individuals, even artists, could not be immune from the impact of political events. The world was claiming her attention and eroding the idealistic individualism of the 1930s and 1940s. In restrospect she confessed: *I was at that time quite simply an intellectual snob, caring only that my work should break through to an élite* (in an early draft of ALUN LEWIS AND THE MAKING OF THE CASEG BROADSHEETS, in the possession of Alan Clodd). Tragically her new awareness came in time to reveal only ugliness, brutality, and betrayal, driving her back into brooding isolation.

POEMS WITH DRAWINGS (1969) – published as a signed limited edition of 200 copies – contains seventeen poems spanning a wide period of Brenda Chamberlain's life. 'When he was cast up', 'Someday', and 'Yesterday I thought' are all from THE GREEN HEART. The first appeared as early as 1945 in TRANSFORMATION, as 'Young Fisher Brought to

Land'. The later poems are mainly adapted from THE PROTAGONISTS and from A ROPE OF VINES. The poems and drawings from the book together formed the substance of the 'Word and Image' exhibition.

POEMS WITH DRAWINGS, like THE GREEN HEART, was dedicated to Karl von Laer. 'Someday' and 'Yesterday I thought' come from the later sections of 'The Green Heart' cycle. 'Someday' expresses a sense of resignation to separation, in life as in death. But more importantly it introduces the concept of rebirth – life out of death – represented both by the trees which grow over the graves, and by her poems. She comes to terms with loneliness and death by apprehending life's continuity through the renewal of nature and the survival of true ideas in art.

Significantly, in 'When he was cast up' one word has been changed from the earlier version. The young fisher surfaces no longer by *the Islands of the Dead*, but *the islands of the Sun*, so that the image of his arrival in a Hades-like region of departed souls is transformed into his return to the world of the living, where he is revived in the memories of those who discover him.

Despite their wide time span, none of the poems is out of key. Stylistically, her later poetry became less dense, and often clipped and rhetorical. The three early works are comparatively simple, yet powerful. Although these verses have no formal pattern, they are bonded by a lilting repetition of sounds and subtle rhythms.

'Father Seraphimou', 'A sore place in me' and 'Tethered to the shadow of a carob-tree' all relate to episodes in A ROPE OF VINES. The first is a

71

sympathetically humorous portrait of the hermit of Meteora discovered at the end of the nightmare journey through the mountains. (The poem is entitled 'Meteora' in NLW, MS 21485E.) 'A sore place in me' tells of the pelican, the *pious bird* persecuted by the townspeople. The legend of the *axe-beaked pelekan*, that feeds its young with its own blood, has many literary sources but no known factual basis. Shakespeare's reference to Goneril and Regan as *pelican daughters* in KING LEAR derived from his own anonymous source material and its description of *the Pellican / That kills it selfe, to save her young one's lives*. A ROPE OF VINES was originally titled 'The Pelican', and in the book it is the anguished Leonidas who is openly compared to the innocent *self-wounder*, although the analogy suits the writer and her tortured sensitivity just as well. 'Tethered to the shadow of a carob-tree' questions the nature of divine power; and its early title 'PAN-IC' indicates that the deities are classical, not Christian.

'Shipwrecked Demeter', although written on Bardsey like 'Rose of Lima', shares this classical ethos. Early versions of these two poems are in a notebook of 1955, and appear in TIDE-RACE. Both take up the theme of *death-into-life, darkness overcome by dayspring*. Persephone, Demeter's daughter, was stolen away to the Underworld by Pluto but allowed to return to her *mourning mother* for half the year, to be 'reborn'. Demeter was the earth goddess, and the myth is understood to represent the annual burying of seed before the growth of the crops. The renewal of life is symbolized here by the bust of the ancient goddess – her power *conserved* – raised from the deep by the sponge-fishers.

Rhys Gwyn remarked that Brenda Chamberlain was attracted to Byzantine art and the cave paintings of

Lascaux[1] because they *grasped something timeless and transcended the rigours of passing years.* In these poems too, art vanquishes death, not purely in the object itself, but through its revitalizing impact on the imagination of those who see it. In 'Rose of Lima' the *wave-worn pebble* assumes a similar mystical significance. It is a *jewel* of natural rather than artistic beauty, thrown up by the sea from the *dark cell* where it has been refined by a symbolic death. In TIDE-RACE Brenda Chamberlain describes how the poem was written. Walking on Bardsey on the saint's day, 30 August, she had a *momentary 'vision'* of the ruined abbey *living* again. The stone – probably jasper – was discovered in *a blood-red cave* and dedicated to the feast day.

This power of the imagination to regenerate life is nowhere better articulated than in 'Give me a dry bone', where a lush setting of gardens and fountains is summoned from the sterile bone. For the human imagination is the most potent of all sources of rebirth. Yet in 'I dream too much' we are reminded again that the imagination can also run out of control into a nightmare world.

In 'There is never an end' the poet explores the continuity of life itself, flowing *like wine, / generation into generation:*

> *I die he dies she dies they die, but it is*
> *not death: it is the flower in the rock,*
> *the bird on the winter sea.*

The image was repeated in a contemporary picture:

[1] Her notes on the Lascaux caves are in the NLW.

The Bride enters the Sepulchre of green Mediterranean light and roses grow from the sterile rock.

Brenda Chamberlain's pictures at this time were not naturalistic, although the 'outer' was always present, and she never strayed into abstract expressionism. Starting from the objects around her – shells and stones and wine jars – she worked often for months, as on her poetry, *proposing, discarding and distilling* until she achieved a *pure central symbol.* Alan Twelves described the process as a *relentless and ruthless pursuit of the underlying basic truths behind appearances.* The image of the pebble on page two is one of the most successful. She stressed that the drawings in the book were *not illustration but counterpoint* (in 'The Relationship between Art and Literature'). She was as reluctant to account for this creative process in her art as in her writing, considering it a reaction to experience too *personally emotional* to express in representational forms ('Spectrum' interview on BBC Radio, 20 July 1968).

The other style in the book is the *automatic* technique she developed in response to music or dancing. She executed the sketches *under tremendous tension with a blind point (no ink) rapidly, wildly, and without looking at what I was doing.* The outlines were then brought out with a wax crayon, and the surface polished with a wool sock. 'Genesis' (p. 29) is the best drawing of all, catching the movements of the whirling dancer, his body flowing from one position to another – the whole dance in one image.

The poem opposite it, 'The Dawn-foretelling cock', was written for choreography by Robertus Saragas. In six lines it captures a series of startling images.

The cock's fanfare heralds the appearance of the dancer:

> A man, astonished at the promise of day,
> stepped onto a roof above the town.

He is tremendously alive. *Flinging his arms to keep the stars at bay,* he wards off the all-seeing eyes, the Fates, in a gesture of glorious defiance. He dances *the rite of life and death,* celebrating every aspect of human experience.

This simple, brief poem, counters the despair in THE PROTAGONISTS. It unites the themes of POEMS WITH DRAWINGS and provides a triumphant, affirmative conclusion.

VII

Brenda Chamberlain's wartime correspondence with Alun Lewis maintained a profound significance for her throughout her life. Over a quarter of a century later she wrote in ALUN LEWIS AND THE MAKING OF THE CASEG BROADSHEETS:

Writing now at this far remove, the broadsheets have little value for me; the letters of Alun Lewis have more life than ever.

John Petts tells how the three artists were drawn together by a strong sympathy for each other's work. He noticed Lewis's writing in THE WELSH REVIEW, and felt inspired to illustrate his short story 'The Wanderers'. Only shyness stopped him contacting the poet. Alun Lewis in turn was impressed by their engravings. His first letter arrived at Llanllechid out of the blue in December 1940 and was greeted by Petts and Chamberlain with amazement.

I've wanted to tell you, everytime I've seen any of your work – every time so far – how exciting, how good with life it is,

Lewis declared. The correspondence became three-sided when John Petts went to Surrey. Brenda Chamberlain kept the letters she received before Alun Lewis's death in Burma on 5 March 1944. In December 1969 she sold twenty-nine of his letters to the Welsh Arts Council for £500, and they were placed in the National Library of Wales.

Her first written account of the production of the broadsheets is found in two holograph manuscripts written in 1962: 'How the Caseg Broadsheets began' and 'How I came to illustrate the Ann Jones Broadsheet'. They were also purchased for the National Library at Sotheby's in July 1965, for £52 19s.8d. The first contains much of the text of the later book.

ALUN LEWIS AND THE MAKING OF THE CASEG BROADSHEETS was published as a limited edition of 335 signed copies in March 1970. It comprised extracts from twenty-eight of the letters, linked by brief passages of her own comment and explanation. Alun's mother Gwladys Lewis described it as *an aristocrat among books. It is a volume I am proud to possess.* But a reviewer in THE TIMES LITERARY SUPPLEMENT in June 1970 criticized its brevity and its high price (four guineas):

By standing too strictly on her title Miss Chamberlain has denied her readers both pleasure and instruction.

Alun Lewis was the prime mover of the broadsheet project. But Chamberlain in her commentary tells us little of her own vital role. As the only member of the trio with control over her own life at that time, she took on responsibility for distributing the broad-sheets and handling *a colossal pile of tedious clerical work* (15 February 1942). Crucial decisions about the contents of the sheets were often left to her – a fact acknowledged by Alun Lewis: *it is your work now; no use pretending it's mine; I never did approve of absentee directors* (15 February 1942).

Yet in limiting her own retrospective comments on

their relationship, Brenda Chamberlain allows the letters to speak for themselves, offering a warm and vivid portrait of the sensitive and uncompromisingly idealistic young soldier poet. The tone of the letters is natural and conversational, tracing a relationship tentatively established almost entirely through the written word:

This sounds carping; you know it isn't, Brenda, don't you? I'm proud of co-operating with you, and overjoyed at our friendship. Because of that, I must give my critical bent its fling, so's you can get to know and like or dislike me, if you choose . . .
(15 February 1942)

Although John Petts was able to meet Alun Lewis on a number of occasions in England, Brenda Chamberlain saw him only once, when the trio spent an intense night together at Llanllechid, walking the hills in the moonlight to show Lewis the Afon Caseg *glimmering with florins* (18 November 1941), and talking round the fire until dawn.

In his letters Brenda Chamberlain sensed a *neurotic questioning, and a need for reassurance. The artist is accustomed to swing from the abyss to the height,* she wrote, when in the late 1960s she was herself besieged by periods of bleak despair. In Lewis's later letters she detected him *becoming more and more isolated,* and commented in a letter of 26 March 1969: *Poor Alun's death-wish came over stronger and stronger.*

It was an *unlikely partnership.* In contrast to Brenda Chamberlain's individualism, Alun Lewis was

moving in a different direction – to a closer mixing with society, with poverty and politics and economics, for I see no other lasting way of creating a situation where Art can live IN THE PEOPLE (14 April 1941).

The broadsheets were intended to revive the seventeenth-century tradition of popular ballad sheets circulated cheaply to farms and villages by peddlers. Although they were committed to the project, Petts and Chamberlain were sceptical about its feasibility: *we thought Alun's belief that we could capture the ears and eyes and pockets of the multitude was a fallacy.*

Distribution difficulties and wartime shortages of paper dogged the Caseg Broadsheets. Production costs escalated, and the original price of one shilling and ninepence for five was repeatedly adjusted.

In a letter of 9 April 1942 Alun Lewis concluded: *we haven't realised the ideal we envisaged at the start, typographically, artistically or poetically.* Brenda Chamberlain found his disappointment justified, and this low evaluation of the broadsheets runs through her commentary:

Broadsheets – a broadside – the tradition has been lost, and I'm afraid our venture did nothing to revive it. These letters are what gave life to what we were trying to do.

Broadsheet five, with Brenda Chamberlain's illustration to part of Dylan Thomas's 'In Memory of Ann Jones', was particularly controversial. Alun Lewis, having had high expectations, disliked it; although Thomas's friend Vernon Watkins found it *really beautiful*; and John Rolph used it in DYLAN THOMAS: A BIBLIOGRAPHY, believing it deserved *almost world-wide circulation.*

The surviving broadsheets, four featuring Chamberlain's work, are now highly prized. Several sets, hand-coloured by John Petts, were sold in New York. But for Brenda Chamberlain they were worthless – *they lay around the house, and their backs were used by children for their drawings, and then thrown away* ('How the Caseg Broadsheets began'). When she left Ynys Enlli she threw the Caseg wood blocks into the sea (letter to Alan Clodd, 30 March 1964).

Alun Lewis's letters had an altogether different significance. In 1945 she wrote:

I feel, and in no derogatory sense, that in passing of time, Alun Lewis will be honoured even more as a man than as a poet. When extracts from his many letters are given in book form to the world, then only will his joyous vitality and sense of responsibility towards men be fully realized.

(THE DUBLIN MAGAZINE)

She believed his letters and the short story 'The Orange Grove' were the finest things he wrote, compared with *something contrived* about his poems, *a shade too much 'poetry'.* Yet she sent many of her own poems to him for assessment. The letters are full of his encouragement and detailed advice. She heeded his counsel, for instance, in transposing the last lines of 'Dead Ponies' (2 June 1941). *I pondered and pondered about the alterations you suggested,* she wrote back (2 July 1941).

In editing the letters for publication, Brenda Chamberlain omitted many of these details, modestly excluding passages in which Alun Lewis enthusiastically praised her work. In April 1941 he wrote about her engraving: *I think you are a great artist. I'm sorry if that upsets you.*

Although he described her poetry as *not as sure and masterly as your engravings,* he showed much admiration for it. *Both of you surpass any other woman poet I've read,* he wrote of Brenda Chamberlain and Lynette Roberts in November 1941. And a month later:

Horizon would like to see your poems, Brenda: I told Connolly you were more important than Anne Ridler or Kay Raine and he raised his worldly brows!

Her editing also demonstrates that she felt there were still private elements in the correspondence which she was unwilling to open to public scrutiny. Not surprisingly, perhaps, she omitted his response to the news of her break with John Petts, and also most of Alun Lewis's references to Gweno and his family.

Other omissions in this brief book are more puzzling, and beg many questions. Why was there no contribution to the story from John Petts, who at that time was living and working in Llansteffan in south Wales? According to Petts (in the 1983 Radio Wales lecture, 'Welsh Horizons'), not only did he design many of the broadsheet images, he also *guided Brenda's hand* on the engraver's tool. On 25 June 1941 he wrote from Addlestead urging her:

Look, there's one thing that's made for you, – one of the early Welsh things, I mean, for you to illustrate. Please, please get going on it now.

How strange that Brenda had written to Alun Lewis just ten days earlier volunteering a design for the same piece.

In truth, their parting was a bitter one. Brenda

Chamberlain changed her *emotional direction* and turned to building her own life and career, claimed John Petts. In 1944 he volunteered for the Royal Army Medical Corps, and undertook dangerous missions with 224 Parachute Field Ambulance. He wrote to Brenda asking for a reconciliation, but, whatever the reason, he did not receive a reply. After that they had little contact, and when Petts became Assistant Director of the Welsh Committee of the Arts Council of Great Britain in 1951 their relationship remained *guarded*.

While writing ALUN LEWIS AND THE MAKING OF THE CASEG BROADSHEETS Brenda Chamberlain wrote to Petts asking for permission to quote from some of his letters to her, and also those from Alun Lewis to him. She also wanted to include three letters he still had: the first one, from Hampshire, dated 20 December 1940; one sent on the way to India in November/December 1942; and one from India on 28 April 1943; and she offered to send back Petts's letters in return.

In 1968 she wrote to the Director of Enitharmon Press, Alan Clodd, asserting that Petts had agreed; and in March 1969 stated that his letters had been sent off, but no reply received. Alan Clodd also wrote twice to John Petts, who confirmed that he failed to respond, and so Alan Clodd eventually omitted three letters from Petts to Chamberlain (15 and 21 April 1941 and 25 June 1941) and three from Lewis to Petts (2 June 1941, June 1941 and 9 July 1941) from the book. Those letters were retained by John Petts. Joan Rees thought that Brenda Chamberlain kept three letters for herself when she sold the others to the Arts Council, but none have so far come to light.

The letters themselves set an even more intriguing puzzle. For their text often varies from Brenda Chamberlain's version in the book. Admittedly Alun Lewis's writing is small and not always clear, and in some places she certainly misread it: in the penultimate letter *wilted* should read *withered* for example. Elsewhere she has corrected grammatical or spelling errors. But on top of these there are casual alterations of a word or phrase which add nothing, and sometimes lose the distinctive flavour of Lewis's style. Many of them are detailed by Roland Mathias in POETRY WALES (Vol.X.iii).

The evidence of Brenda Chamberlain's own typescript and galley proofs – in the hands of Alan Clodd – suggest some of these changes were made in the writing and others in the printing. The switch from *cheeryble* to *cheerful* (January 1942), for instance, was made by Brenda Chamberlain. By contrast, in the letter of 26 July 1942 Brenda left Alun Lewis's *orifices*, and the amended *offices* in the proofs was never corrected. The apparent arbitrariness of the editing is illustrated by the November 1941 letter. A printer's error left the sentence *That is the great truth through which you must create through.* In her proofs Brenda Chamberlain, instead of deleting the first 'through' in line with Lewis's text, crossed out the last one.

Sometimes Brenda Chamberlain's misreading of the letters has a serious impact on their meaning. Lewis's letter of February 1942 should read:

I suggest that your imagery and the words that express it are reaching the stage where they must change and grow and become something wider, deeper and more sinuous-reaching in their roots, less 'oppressed by mountains'. Also that you will discarded [sic] *'flat' words such as 'tinctured'. Rilke, even in translation, is a rich source of words for the same fundamental thoughts as you work in. It is only a kind of preparation . . .*

In the original there is an omission mark after *mountains*, with the next two sentences placed at the top of the page. In the book the phrases are muddled incomprehensibly.

The order of the letters is even more confusing. The three lines printed by themselves on page 26 do not come from a lost letter, as Roland Mathias speculates. All Alun Lewis's other letters of that month come from Aberdare, and not from Woodbridge in Suffolk, as this supposedly did. The three lines are in fact printed again in ALUN LEWIS AND THE MAKING OF THE CASEG BROADSHEETS in their correct place: as part of a letter of March 1942 from Ipswich (p. 33). The PS added, in the book, to the October 1941 letter (p. 18), actually followed an earlier one that is dated in the book as 25 April 1941, from Heysham Towers in Lancashire. This dating itself is wrong – on the letter the month can be distinguished as August 1941. Earlier that year Lewis was in Hampshire, not Lancashire. In Alan Clodd's notes a timetable of Lewis's movements between June 1940 and October 1942 places him in Hampshire until June 1941.

The most important and astonishing inaccuracy comes at the end of the book. In the last pages Brenda Chamberlain describes the *long letter* written to her on 7 February 1944 – the last she received. In fact, large portions of the letter printed under this date were included in the previous one of 3 October

1943. All the second half of the 'last' letter, starting from *I want to wish you fortitude and independence of spirit* forms part of the October letter in the National Library of Wales. The letter of 7 February 1944 ends after the reference to HA! HA! AMONG THE TRUMPETS.

Roland Mathias has discussed the difference in the tone of the two letters and why their true order is important. How did such a glaring error occur? Did Brenda Chamberlain deliberately manipulate the dating to give the story a more suitable ending – another example of 'inventing' life? For in the book Alun Lewis's last words form a sort of epilogue:

Well, Brenda, God bless you. I hope we meet again some time . . . I hope to see you both say in 1948 or 9. I don't expect to be home earlier, if ever.

Or were there other motives? Was she attempting to protect Alun Lewis, knowing perhaps of his relationship with Freda Aykroyd (see John Pikoulis, ALUN LEWIS – A LIFE, Poetry Wales Press, 1984), or fearing new speculation that he committed suicide? Or was she guarding the privacy of her own tribulations with John Petts?

The evidence shows that Brenda Chamberlain was confused over the order of the letters. She was desperately anxious to see the book published, but at that time was deeply involved in rehearsals for THE PROTAGONISTS, haggling over the sale of manuscripts to ease her financial problems, and preparing art exhibitions. Before the work was completed she suffered her nervous breakdown.

The Daedalus Press in Norfolk, which printed ALUN

LEWIS AND THE MAKING OF THE CASEG BROADSHEETS, went out of business around 1983, and no final typescript is available. The one in Alan Clodd's possession bears little relation to the book, having few dates, longer extracts from the letters, and little commentary. He was acting as Chamberlain's bibliographical adviser, and she sent him copies of the letters hoping for help in dating them. A great deal of correspondence over the order still exists, but little evidence of how decisions were reached. In August 1968 Clodd wrote to her with his own suggested redating. In September 1969 when Brenda Chamberlain received proofs of the book she wrote back: *one of the letters is in wrong order and that must be my mistake, I suppose.*

In March 1969 Gweno Lewis herself wrote to Alan Clodd suggesting the reordering of four pages. One of them was a letter to John Petts, subsequently omitted; but it is impossible to identify the others. In the early typescript, in which the letters are arranged quite haphazardly, the section of the October 1943 letter which was subsequently misplaced is found immediately after the airgraph of 21 February 1943, as if it were part of the same letter; not at the end as in the book.

Furthermore, Brenda Chamberlain stated that there were twenty-seven letters, when there are twenty-eight in the book, and twenty-nine in the National Library; since one, dated *Tuesday* and written in summer 1942, is excluded from the book altogether, and looks as if its first page(s) has been lost or kept back. Yet it is significant that the last letters are the most clearly dated of all. The *I wish you fortitude* passage is directly under an unmistakable date-line.

It is impossible to believe that there was a simple error on Brenda Chamberlain's part, but we may never know what was in her mind.

Alun Lewis's death left Brenda Chamberlain *utterly stunned and bereft*, she told Seumas O'Sullivan, editor of THE DUBLIN MAGAZINE. He published her memorial article and her review of the poetry collection HA! HA! AMONG THE TRUMPETS, in which she tells movingly how she first read lines from 'The Sentry' in Lewis's letter of 14 April 1941,

in the street, with rain falling like tears and puckering the page . . . I was to know through friendship the development of his gifts as man and poet.

In her poem 'For Alun',[1] she brings true the haunting pledge in his last letter: *I'll come walking the hills with you in flesh or ghost, surely I will.* She pictures the *sweet singing spirit* leaving *the orange grove* on its mystical pilgrimage:

Slowly returning on our tidal tears.
The homing spirit smiles through mountain rain,
Throws war's dirt from him
In the barren lake;
Becomes complete.

[1] Published in WALES (June 1944) and POETRY CHICAGO (September 1945).

VIII

Brenda Chamberlain's career coincided with a literary renaissance in Wales. In the 1930s, 40s and 50s this country was the seed-ground of a new creative energy, blossoming in a succession of young poets and writers who clearly identified their nationality. The colourful, romantic flamboyance of Dylan Thomas and his contemporaries was inseparable from their Welshness.

In 1949 Kenneth Rexroth placed Chamberlain at the forefront of the 'Welsh school' of poetry, centred on Keidrych Rhys's magazine WALES. He felt that she shared with other women poets – Anne Ridler, Kathleen Raine, Lynette Roberts and Denise Levertov – a more personal, imaginative mode of expression, used to deal with intimate themes.

Brenda Chamberlain developed alongside writers like Dylan Thomas, and Glyn Jones, whose work captures the distinctive characteristics of Welsh life. Yet despite the many Welsh influences in her writing, she fits uneasily into Jones's definition of Anglo-Welsh writers as *those Welshmen who write in English about Wales* (THE DRAGON HAS TWO TONGUES, J. M. Dent, 1968). She was Welsh by birth only, not by ancestry; and much of her writing was not *about Wales*. More importantly, her ambition was to get

through the narrow archway of the enchanted castle that is

Wales into the no less enchanted universe outside, of which the castle and its inhabitants are part.
(Brenda Chamberlain's review of
THE BUTTERCUP FIELD AND OTHER STORIES by Gwyn Jones.
THE DUBLIN MAGAZINE, April 1946).

Wales was her springboard. Even in TIDE-RACE, she explored her Welsh environment only to discover more widely relevant truths about human life. Yet it was Wales that inspired her best writing, and brought her most personal happiness.

She had no desire to 'sell' Wales to the rest of the world. The privacy of the places she loved, such as Ynys Enlli and Llanllechid, was jealously guarded. Nor did she have any sympathy at all for the idea of a self-contained, 'preserved' Welsh culture. Considering the 'Anglo-Welsh story' in 1946 she declared:

Until the tale is made universal, rooted maybe in locality, but reaching out to the full stretch of man's spirit, there will be more than the stalemate that has begun to show itself in Anglo-Welsh letters. There will be decadence and corruption where, not so long ago, was renaissance.

The pervading ethos of her work is Celtic rather than specifically Welsh, characterized, in her words, by the *close juxtaposition* of the *earthly-material and the supernatural.* Wales endowed her with a *rich heritage* in its strength of tradition and spirit. After TIDE-RACE, when the place-names changed their sound, the fatalistic Celtic *Weltanschauung* remained the same.

Brenda Chamberlain read widely and was certainly influenced by other writers – some Welsh, some not.

Alun Lewis detected echoes of D. H. Lawrence and the Bible in her poetry. Yet she remained a solitary figure. Kyffin Williams described her as a *great personality* whose work was *intensely personal*, and therefore unlikely to influence others:

Nevertheless she will always be admired as an artist of unusual talent who allowed us to glimpse into a world of aesthetic purity of which we would have been entirely unaware.

She urged Anglo-Welsh writers to *explore the labyrinth, dive into the wells of the secret heart*, and that was her own aspiration.

John Petts believed that Brenda Chamberlain never fully developed her genius. *I don't often use that word,* he added. Yet TIDE-RACE, as Conran points out, is *a minor classic of Anglo-Welsh literature*, and merits immortality.

Brenda Chamberlain is as well, if not better known for her painting as her writing. In 'The Relationship between Art and Literature' she describes how she was attracted by both forms of expression, but felt compelled by the *art dealer's world* to make a choice for fear of *falling between two stools*. With characteristic fatalism she sought *a sign from heaven*. She elected to train as a painter, but found she turned to writing during periods of *unhappiness*.

Although the two forms were closely related throughout her life, they rarely flowed together. The catalogue for 'Two Painters' explains:

The emotions which control her writing are not those which may be contained in painting, and it is only by using now the medium of writing, now of painting that she has been able to extend the range of her awareness of the world around her.

A pattern emerged of periods of writing alternating with periods of painting. In between lay painful interludes of struggling for expression and *feeling only half alive.*

Brenda Chamberlain created herself as an artist through sustained hard work and never lost awareness of herself in that role. She 'invented her own life', fervently believing it to be something unique and remarkable, and making it so in her writing. The world was a perpetual source of wonder to her, and her acute sensitivity to every aspect of life was never dulled, for she used her imagination to escape from ugliness and routine, and to fashion a more meaningful vision of truth. In THE DOORS OF PERCEPTION Aldous Huxley recognized that:

Men have attached more importance to the inscape than to objective existents, have felt that what they saw with their eyes shut possessed a spiritually higher significance than what they saw with their eyes open. The reason? Familiarity breeds contempt, and how to survive is a problem ranging in urgency from the chronically tedious to the excruciating.

In her life's design, Brenda Chamberlain occasionally, in the words of Eliot's FOUR QUARTETS, *imposed* a pattern that *falsified.* But she was able, too, to apprehend the pattern that is *new in every moment, a new and shocking / Valuation of all we have been.*

Inevitably, the notable experiences that sparked her imagination came to an end, and later in life she turned more frequently to images from the past. It was the unendurable, nagging ache of survival which, imposing itself on her, destroyed her. Back in her prosaically familiar home town of Bangor, deprived of spiritual exaltation, she could not sustain her role as an artist. Her art and her living were one – neither could survive without the other. In her essay on A. E. Housman, Chamberlain wrote:

If we study art and men we find that those great souls who are most conscious of death are most aware of the essence of vitality also. When a man wants most powerfully to live then he will know the bitter watchfulness of death.

Her preoccupation with death was shared by many of the writers she most admired. In her posthumous tribute she said of Alun Lewis:

Men that love life, holding it with passion, have often strong foreknowledge of death . . .

'The act of consecration to death is a sort of flowering, as if the flower should find a voice and say, "This is my blossom, it is red",' said Robert Nichols.

Brenda Chamberlain herself held life *with passion.* Every perception of its overwhelming beauty was a reminder of its transience. She struggled to come to terms with it, to fearlessly embrace death so that she, like her dark-eyed fishermen, could live consummately. She must have endorsed Rilke's words, referring to his DUINO ELEGIES:

Affirmation of life AND affirmation of death reveal themselves as one. To concede the one without the other is, as is here experienced and celebrated, a restriction that finally excludes all infinity.

('Briefe aus Muzot', to Witold von Hulewicz,
13 November 1925).

Yet still the unremitting pain, the growing sense of loss inflicted by life filled her with *pitiable despair*. She cast around for sources of consolation: rebirth through art, nature or the imagination; or the continuity of life in history. She certainly confided her *tragic feeling* to Karl von Laer. In his letter from Schlotheim in 1933, Franz writes to Elizabeth:

. . . look at the flowers and shrubs and trees. Do you mean that they grow and bloom obeying a dark constraint depressed with melancholy, and not rather attached to life?

O dear – this life is beautiful, though sometimes clouds cover the ray-eye of God . . .

Do not grieve that one day you must die. After good work done it is time to sleep. That is not tragic but natural.

These words form the nucleus of Brenda Chamberlain's most valiant reconciliation of life and death in 'The Green Heart' Part I.iii.

In my view she never did come to terms with her own mortality, and as she grew older her anguish grew more intense. The bold, conscious confrontation of destiny is very different from self-annihilation, which often expresses fear and desperation. Brenda Chamberlain's final, fatal gesture was a plea for life, not a reconciliation with death.

Perhaps the key to understanding her work is provided again by Rilke, who wrote to Clara in October 1907:

You notice . . . how necessary it was to get beyond even love; it comes naturally to you to love each one of these things . . . but if you shew it, you make them less well; you judge them instead of saying them. You cease being impartial; and love, the best thing of all, remains outside your work, does not enter into it, is left over unresolved beside it.

Brenda Chamberlain's writing did show her love for people and places; and was sometimes made 'less well' as a result. She might have profited from a little more humour and detachment, a little less earnestness; but that would not have been Brenda Chamberlain.

She bound her life and literature into one unique and exalting vision. In November 1941, Alun Lewis defined her way:

There is no other Brenda Chamberlain living – and I don't think there has been one ever before. That is the great truth you must create through.

A Selected Bibliography

In the scope of this essay it has not been possible to refer in detail to the wide and fascinating selection of Brenda Chamberlain's manuscripts and unpublished work in the National Library of Wales. This includes her notebooks (1930s–1960s); THE PROTAGONISTS; 'How the Caseg Broadsheets began'; 'A One-legged Man takes a Walk' (unfinished) and 'The Monument' (unfinished); prose and poetry drafts; and exhibition catalogues. Alun Lewis's letters are also in the National Library (MS 20798C).

BRENDA CHAMBERLAIN

THE GREEN HEART, Oxford University Press, 1958.

TIDE-RACE, Hodder and Stoughton, 1962. Republished by Seren Books, 1987.

THE WATER-CASTLE, Hodder and Stoughton, 1964.

A ROPE OF VINES, Hodder and Stoughton, 1965.

POEMS WITH DRAWINGS, Enitharmon Press, 1969.

ALUN LEWIS AND THE MAKING OF THE CASEG BROADSHEETS, Enitharmon Press, 1970.

Periodical Contributions and Essays

'Abstract of a Journey 1962', MABON, Summer 1970.

ARTISTS IN WALES, ed. Meic Stephens, Gwasg Gomer, 1971.

'Childhood', THE DUBLIN MAGAZINE, April–June 1947.

'From a Journal', LIFE AND LETTERS, May 1945, September 1946 and October 1946.

'From Other Hills', THE WELSH REVIEW, November 1939 (with John Petts).

'Mountains of Rock', THE WELSH REVIEW, September 1945.

'The Return', LIFE AND LETTERS, August 1947, and THE PENGUIN BOOK OF WELSH SHORT STORIES, ed. Alun Richards, 1976.

'A Total Eclipse of the Sun', MABON, Spring 1972.

Some Uncollected Poems

'Being by Nature Unaware', ST MARY'S HOSPITAL GAZETTE, May 1962.

'Bird, Flower and Vermin', ST MARY'S HOSPITAL GAZETTE, March/April 1962.

'Blodeuwedd', POETRY LONDON X, December 1944, and WALES, December 1946.

'Give No White Flower', THE BELL, November 1942, and NEW IRISH POETS, 1948.

'Hay-Carrying: Enlli', MABON, Spring 1969.

'He Sat by the Shore of a Lake', THE DUBLIN MAGAZINE, July 1941.

'The House of Fishes, Trees and Birds', featured in Gimpel Fils exhibition of work by Scottie Wilson.

'In Old Age', NEW YORK TIMES, 20 July 1961; ST MARY'S HOSPITAL GAZETTE, May 1962, and NEW YORK TIMES BOOK OF VERSE, 1970.

'Irish Sea', MABON, Spring 1969.

'It is Fear I Have of Returning', THE DUBLIN MAGAZINE, July 1941.

'Poem for Five Airmen', THE WELSH REVIEW, March 1944.

'Slowly, Spring Begins', ST MARY'S HOSPITAL GAZETTE, March/April 1962.

'Tryfan', THE DUBLIN MAGAZINE, July 1941.

'Voices Speak from the Crevasse', POETRY QUARTERLY, Winter 1943.

'Would it not Move to Pity', THE DUBLIN MAGAZINE, July 1941.

Other Publications

THE MAGIC JOURNEY by Dora Broome, illustrated by Brenda Chamberlain, University of London Press, 1960.

Criticism

Anthony Conran, 'The Writings of Brenda Chamberlain', ANGLO-WELSH REVIEW, Spring 1972; and THE COST OF STRANGENESS, Gwasg Gomer, 1982.

Tony Conran, FRONTIERS IN ANGLO-WELSH POETRY, University of Wales Press, 1997.

Maurice Cooke, 'The Painting of Brenda Chamberlain', ANGLO-WELSH REVIEW, Spring 1972.

Rhys Gwyn, 'The Art of Brenda Chamberlain', DOCK LEAVES, Autumn 1957.

Kate Holman, 'The Literary Achievement of Brenda Chamberlain', University College of Swansea MA thesis, 1976, including a bibliography of all published poems and prose.

Kate Holman, '"So Near, So Far, Brother or Lover?"', NEW WELSH REVIEW, Autumn 1988.

Roland Mathias, 'The Caseg Letters – a commentary', POETRY WALES, X.iii (1975). Alun Lewis – Special Number.

Jill Piercy, 'Between Two Arts', PLANET, April/May 1988.

Kyffin Williams, 'An Appreciation', MABON, Spring 1972.

Background

John Petts, 'Welsh Horizons', 1983 BBC Radio Wales lecture.

John Pikoulis, ALUN LEWIS – A LIFE, Poetry Wales Press, 1984.

Acknowledgements

I am indebted to a large number of people who, over a period of more than twelve years, took the time to talk to me about Brenda Chamberlain. Sadly, they are too numerous to mention individually here, and, indeed, over the intervening years some have died. Nevertheless, I should like to record my special thanks to John Petts, Karl von Laer, Joan Rees and Alan Clodd; and also to Neville and Dorothy Chamberlain and Gweno Lewis.

I am grateful to staff at the National Library of Wales for their help and co-operation, and to Meic Stephens for his advice. Also to Cecil Price for introducing me to Brenda Chamberlain's work, and to Gwyn Jones for his timely encouragement. Finally, this work is dedicated to David and George Peters of Ammanford, Dyfed, who brought me to Wales and taught me to love it, and to the memory of Mary Peters.

The Author

Kate Holman was born in London in 1951. Her father was a Londoner and her mother Irish. She studied English and Philosophy at Southampton University, and went on to University College Swansea where she completed an MA thesis on the writing of Brenda Chamberlain. In 1973–4 she lived for a year in Sicily, teaching English; and on returning to England, trained as a journalist. For seven years she was a regular London correspondent for the Dublin IRISH PRESS group of newspapers and a freelance contributor to many other journals and publications including the GUARDIAN and the NEW STATESMAN. In 1988 she moved to Brussels, Belgium, where she worked for the European Commission as an expert consultant on women and the media, and completed research for UNICEF on media ethics and children. She still lives and works in Brussels with her two children, Beatrice and Patrick.

Designed by Jeff Clements
Typesetting at the University of Wales Press in
11pt Palatino and printed in Great Britain by
Dinefwr Press, Llandybïe, 1997

British Library Cataloguing in Publication Data.
A catalogue record for this book is available from the
British Library.

ISBN 0-7083-1048-6

The Publishers wish to acknowledge the financial
assistance of the Arts Council of Wales towards the cost
of producing this volume.